Facts abou W9-BYW-817

Published by the Department of Foreign Affairs, Dublin
Designed by Elizabeth Fitz-Simon Murray
Cover design by Bill Murphy
Printed in Ireland by Irish Printers Limited

Fifth edition

DUBLIN 1981

Cover: The Shrine of St Patrick's Bell, C. 1100 AD, from the
collection of the National Museum of Ireland (Photo:
Brendan Doyle, NMI).

ISBN 0 906404 10 X (hardback)
ISBN 0 906404 12 6 (paperback)

Contents

Contents

Introduction

The object of this booklet is to give a general overview of the economic, social and cultural life of Ireland, its history and governmental structure. It is designed mainly for people abroad with an interest in Ireland. While the material in the booklet is intended to cover the most important areas of Irish life, it is not possible in the short space available to include everything. The short bibliography given at the end is intended as an indication as to where fuller treatments of the areas may be found.

Except where otherwise stated, the material in this booklet relates to the independent twenty-six counties area of Ireland.

Land and People

Counties and Provinces

Provincial Boundaries
County Boundaries
Boundary of
Northern Ireland

DONEGAL
DERRY
ANTRIM
ULSTER
TYRONE
DOWN
FERMANAGH
ARMAGH
LEITRIM
MONAGHAN
SLIGO
CAVAN
LOUTH
MAYO
CONNACHT
ROSCOMMON
LONGFORD
MEATH
WESTMEATH
GALWAY
DUBLIN
OFFALY
KILDARE
LEINSTER
LAOIS
WICKLOW
CLARE
KILKENNY
CARLOW
TIPPERARY
LIMERICK
WEXFORD
MUNSTER
KERRY
WATERFORD
CORK

Scale 1:3,000,000

30 20 10 0   30   60 Km

30   20   10   0   30 Miles

Prepared at the Ordnance Survey Dublin
© Government of Ireland 1978

Physical Features

The island of Ireland is situated in the extreme north-west of the continent of Europe between 51½° and 55½° north latitude and 5½° and 10½° west longitude.

The Irish Sea to the east, which separates Ireland from Britain, is from 11 to 120 miles (17.6 to 320 km) wide and less than 650 feet (200 metres) deep. In other areas the shallow waters of the Continental Shelf are rather narrow and depths increase rapidly into the Atlantic Ocean.

Total Area	32,595 sq. miles (84,421 sq. km)
Ireland (Republic)	27,136 sq. miles (70,282 sq. km)
Northern Ireland	5,459 sq. miles (14,139 sq. km)
Greatest length (N-S)	302 miles (486 km)
Greatest width (E-W)	171 miles (275 km)
Total coastline	1,970 miles (3,173 km)

The island comprises a large central lowland of limestone with a relief of hills girded by a discontinuous border of coastal mountains which vary greatly in geological structure.

The mountain ridges of the south are parallel east-west foldings of old red sandstone separated by limestone river valleys. Granite predominates in the mountains of Galway, Mayo and Donegal in the west and north-west and in counties Down and Wicklow on the east coast, while a basalt plateau covers much of the north-east of the country. The central plain, which is broken in places by low hills, is extensively covered with glacial deposits of clay and sand. It has considerable areas of bog and numerous lakes.

Ireland has seen at least two general glaciations and everywhere ice-smoothed rock, mountain lakes, glacial valleys and deposits of glacial sand, gravel and clay mark the passage of the ice.

Topography

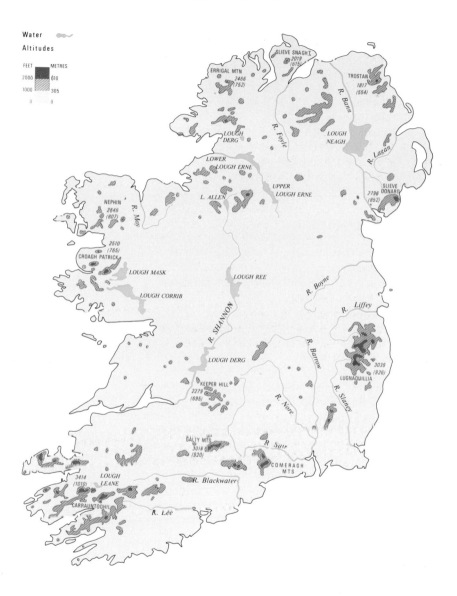

Water

Altitudes

FEET	METRES
2000	610
1000	305
0	0

SLIEVE SNAGH.T.
2019
(615)

ERRIGAL MTN
2466
(752)

TROSTAN
1817
(554)

R. Bann

R. Foyle

LOUGH
DERG

LOUGH
NEAGH

R. Lagan

LOWER
LOUGH ERNE

UPPER
LOUGH ERNE

SLIEVE
DONARD
2796
(852)

NEPHIN
2846
(807)

L. ALLEN

R. Moy

2510
(765)
CROAGH PATRICK

LOUGH MASK

LOUGH REE

R. Boyne

R. Liffey

LOUGH CORRIB

R. SHANNON

LOUGH DERG

KEEPER HILL
2279
(695)

R. Barrow

LUGNAQUILLIA
3039
(926)

R. Slaney

R. Nore

GALTY MTS
3018
(920)

R. Suir

COMERAGH
MTS

3414
(1010)
LOUGH
LEANE

R. Blackwater

CARRAUNTOOHIL

R. Lee

Scale 1:3,000,000

30 20 10 0   30   60 Km

30   20   10   0   30 Miles

Prepared at the Ordnance Survey Dublin

© Government of Ireland 1978

Climate

Ireland lies in an area of mild south-westerly winds and comes under the influence of the warm drifting waters of the Gulf Stream. This has assured it an equable climate and, as the island is comparatively small with no part more than seventy miles from the sea, temperature is almost uniform over the country.

Average air temperatures in January and February, the coldest months, are mainly between 4°C and 7°C. July and August, the two warmest months, have average temperatures between 14°C and 16°C, but occasionally reaching as high as 25°C.

Rainfall is well distributed, with the west, because of the prevailing winds from the Atlantic, having a higher annual rainfall than the east, where it is as low as 30 inches (75 centimetres) a year. Snow is relatively infrequent except in the mountains. When it does occur, it is rarely prolonged or severe.

The sunniest months are May and June with an average sunshine duration of between 5½ and 6½ hours per day over most of the country. The extreme southeast is the sunniest area with an average daily duration of about 7½ hours in May and June and over 6 hours in July and August.

During winter months, Ireland keeps to Greenwich Mean Time, but from April to October, daylight saving time or 'summer time' is in operation and clocks are kept one hour in advance of GMT.

Rainfall

ANNUAL AMOUNT

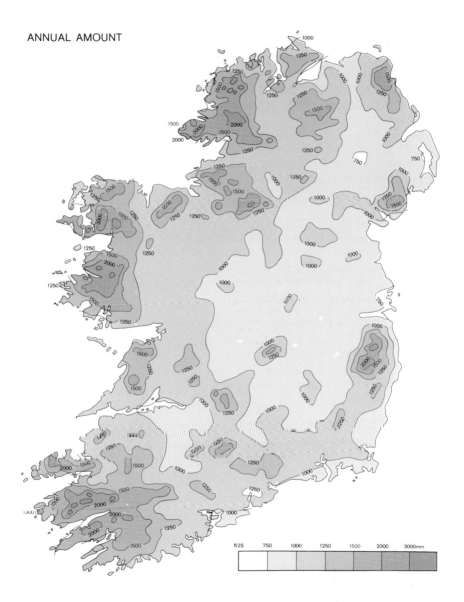

625 750 1000 1250 1500 2000 3000mm

Scale 1:3,000,000

30 20 10 0   30   60 Km

30   20   10   0   30 Miles

Prepared at the Ordnance Survey Dublin

© Government of Ireland 1978

Flora and Fauna

Ireland's separation from the European mainland occurred in the period following the last ice-age in which much of the earlier fauna perished. As a result the flora and fauna of Ireland encompass a smaller range than elsewhere in Europe.

There exists a variety of soils in Ireland, reflecting the complex bedrock geology and the repeated glaciation during the last ice-age.

Although the original forests have been cleared over most of the country, survivals of the old natural forest indicate that forests of oak interspersed with holly and birch predominated, with ash, hazel and yew forests occurring in limestone areas. These were very rich in lichens, mosses, liverworts and ferns. In recent decades the re-afforestation programme has favoured Sitka spruce, Scots, contorta and other pines, larches, Norway spruce and Douglas fir.

Raised peat bogs, varying in size from a couple of acres to a few square miles, occur in the Central Plain in areas of impeded drainage while mountain bogs are common in western areas with heavy rainfall. The flora of the bogs consist of a large variety of bog-moss species together with heather and sedges. Two especially interesting botanical areas are Killarney and Glengariff (Cork/Kerry) which are very rich in bryophytes and lichen species of extreme oceanic and even tropical distribution. The Burren in Co. Clare is a region of bare carboniferous limestone, containing arctic-alpine species surviving from the last glaciation and Mediterranean species at the northern end of their range.

Of some 380 species of wild birds recorded in Ireland, 135 breed in the country. There is considerable migration of birds to Ireland in spring and autumn, while winter migration brings a number of species from Greenland and Iceland. Three-quarters of the world population of the Greenland Whitefronted Goose winter in Ireland. The significance of this has been marked by the establishment of an

2
3
4

5
6
7

8
9
10

11
12
13

16

2. Heather (Erica tetralix).

3. Gorse (Ulex europaeus).

4. Dog Violet (Viola riviniana).

5. Bird's foot Trefoil (Lotus corniculatus).

6. Mountain Avens (Dryas octopetala).

7. Early Purple Orchid (Orchis mascula).

8. Sea Pink (Armeria maritima).

9. Lady's Bedstraw, yellow flower (Galium verum); Eyebright, white flower (Euphrasia sp.).

10. Bracken (Pteridium aquilinum).

11. Bottlebrush (Calistemon), a native of Australia.

12. Water Lily (Nymphaea alba).

13. Bluebells (Hyacinthoides non-scriptus).

14. Peacock Butterfly (Inachis io).

15. Chaffinch (Fringilla coelebs).

16. Skylark (Alauda arvensis).

Continued on page 19

14
15

16
17

18
19

20
21

Flora and Fauna

internationally important Wildlife Reserve in Co. Wexford. There is also considerable passage migration from the south by birds who nest further north. Game shooting is strictly controlled and, in addition, there is a national network of refuges where all game shooting is prohibited. Some wild game bird stocks — mainly pheasant and mallard duck — are augmented through State-assisted restocking programmes. Inland waters support colonies of swans, geese, waders, duck, tern and gulls.

The woods harbour many species such as blackbirds, song thrushes, goldcrests, chaffinches, bullfinches and siskins. Bird life is more sparse on bogs and marshland but includes curlews, snipe, skylarks, gulls, pipits, and geese. The Atlantic coastline, rich in sea food, supports auks, gulls and kestrels, while the estuaries contain flocks of duck, oyster-catchers, wigeons, geese and swans. A large proportion of the world's stormy petrels and gannets breed on the southern and western coasts of Ireland.

Freshwater fishes include salmon, trout, char, pollan and eel. A variety of fishes has been introduced in more recent times, such as pike and rainbow trout. Amphibians are represented in Ireland by a single native species each of frog, toad and newt. Only one native reptile, the common lizard, is found.

Mammals are similar to those found throughout temperate Europe. Several of the thirty-one species are recent introductions. The most interesting examples of native development of variation within the group of Irish mammals are the Irish stoat and the Irish hare. Among domesticated animals, the Irish horse is world famous. There are seven distinctively Irish breeds of dog including the Irish wolfhound.

People

The decline in population as a result of the Great Famine in the 1840s and emigration continued until 1961, since when a steady increase has occurred. Between 1961 and 1979 the population increased by 550,000 from 2,818,000 to 3,368,000. The annual rate of increase between 1971 and 1979 was 1.5%.

The growth of urban population, already considerable in the north-east at the turn of the century, has been more marked in the rest of the island since that date. In 1971, 58.9% of the population lived in towns. This represented an aggregate increase in urban population of 3.5% for the period 1961 — 1971.

In Northern Ireland, the post-Famine population decline has been reversed since the turn of the century. Between 1961 and 1978 the population there increased by 113,800 (or 8%) from 1,425,000 to 1,538,800 (estimated).

In 1975, the average marriage age for males was 27.0 and 24.7 for females. In Northern Ireland, in 1977, it was 25.3 for males and 23.2 for females.

While Ireland has been settled by many different people over the centuries, some widely distributed characteristics can be observed. Over half the population belongs to blood group O (indicating a Nordic strain); about half have blue eyes and a large majority have brown hair. About 4% of the population have red hair.

% Housing stock, 1971, (total 726,300)

Other

Other rented /13

Rented from Local Authority 15.5

Owner occupied 68.8

Religious Denominations (1971)

Denomination	Ireland (Republic)	(%)	Northern Ireland	(%)	Total	(%)
Roman Catholic	2,795,666	(93.9)	477,921	(31.44)	3,273,587	(72.8)
Church of Ireland	97,739	(3.3)	334,318	(22.0)	432,057	(9.6)
Presbyterian	16,052	(0.5)	405,717	(26.7)	421,769	(9.4)
Methodist	5,646	(0.2)	71,235	(4.7)	76,881	(1.7)
Baptist	591	(0.02)	16,563	(1.1)	17,154	(0.4)
Jewish	2,633	(0.08)	959	(0.06)	3,592	(0.1)
Others (incl. no reply)	59,921	(2.0)	212,927	(14.0)	272,848	(6.0)
Total population	2,978,248		1,519,640		4,497,888	

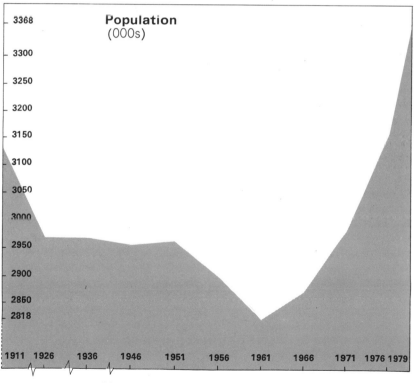

Population (000s)

3368 3300 3250 3200 3150 3100 3050 3000 2950 2900 2850 2818

1911 1926 1936 1946 1951 1956 1961 1966 1971 1976 1979

32. The portal dolmen at Poulnabrone, Co. Clare. This prehistoric stone tomb dates from about 2000 BC.

33. Dún Aengus, on the Aran Island of Inishmore, is one of the most spectacular examples of the Irish stone fort.

History

The earliest inhabitants of Ireland were mesolithic food-gatherers and hunters, who arrived in Antrim after the end of the ice-age The first known existence of them, about 7000 BC, is found in the vicinity of Mount Sandel, near Coleraine. They appear to have lived mainly along coasts and near rivers.

Neolithic settlers with improved tools and a knowledge of agriculture and pottery reached Ireland before 3000 BC. Different waves of settlement are attested by the various modes of burial which now appear. These include some impressive court cairns, portal dolmens and the spectacular complex of megalithic passage graves in the Boyne valley.

Miners and bronze-workers came to Ireland about 2000 BC. These included the Beaker Folk, so known elsewhere in Europe from their distinctive pottery. They in turn were followed in succeeding centuries by other groups of settlers who brought new tools and techniques.

From the earliest times, there is evidence of considerable trade even with distant lands. Stone-age Ireland exported flint and axes while bronze-age Ireland exported gold and manufactured objects in return for raw materials, luxury goods and ornaments.

Iron was brought to Ireland about 300 BC by the Celts, linguistically a branch of the great Indo-European family, who imposed their language and customs on the earlier inhabitants. In successive invasions in the last centuries before Christ, they brought with them their distinctive culture known as La Tène. Their society and laws preserved many archaic features of Indo-European culture.

Early Celtic Ireland was divided into about 150 local kingdoms *(tuatha)* subject to overkings who were in turn under a loose suzerainty of five provincial kings.

History

34. The opening page of St Mark's Gospel from the seventh-century Book of Durrow.

Despite the lack of a central political authority, there was, from the time of the earliest records, a remarkable cultural unity expressed in a standard literary language free of dialect variations in the hands of a professional body of poets, historians and lawgivers, heirs to the pre-Christian druids. Their works survive in the archaic law tracts and epics such as *Táin Bó Cuailnge* which depict early Irish society. This society was based on the extended family *(fine)* in which laws were enforced through an elaborate system of sureties and fines.

Christianity was introduced into Ireland in the fifth century. The work of St Patrick in the latter half of that century contributed greatly to its rapid acceptance and brought the Irish into contact with the world of classical learning. Patrick worked mainly in the northern part of the country with other missionaries, most of whom were probably from the west of Britain.

The organisation of the early Church in Ireland was based on monasteries where a particularly severe discipline was observed rather than, as elsewhere, on a diocesan structure. Some of these monasteries such as Clonmacnoise and Glendalough later became famous centres of learning which attracted large numbers of students from abroad.

Irish monks produced copies of standard Latin texts and first committed the oral Gaelic literature of the Irish Celts to writing. They also produced a lyric poetry of high quality and developed the La Tène artistic tradition in the illumination of their manuscripts while their patronage of craftsmen who produced reliquaries, chalices and croziers furthered the development of the plastic arts in the same style.

At the time when Christianity had become firmly established in Ireland, the Roman Empire had fallen to the barbarians. Irish monks undertook missionary activities throughout north-western Europe and travelled far and wide on the European continent and

INITIUM

euange-
lii ihu xpi

filii di sicut sc
riptum in esa-
ia propheta · ecce mitto an-
gelum meum ante faciem...
tuam qui praeparabit uia(m)
uox clamantis in deser-
to parate uiam dni rec-
tas facite semitas eius ;;
fuit iohannis in deserto
babtizans & praedicans
babtismum paenitentiae
in remisionem peccatoru(m)
& egrediebatur ad illum omnes rege
iudeae regio & hierusolimitae uni
uersi & babtizabantur ab illo in ior
dane flumine confitentes peccata su(a)
& erat iohannis uestitus pilis cam...

35

36

35. An aerial view of
the ruins of the
monastery of
Clonmacnoise.

36. The Basilica of
St Columbanus at
Bobbio, Italy.

History

in Britain. The many monasteries which they established were responsible in no small measure for the preservation of classical culture within the confines of the old Empire and for the conversion of the barbarian tribes there and beyond.

One of the earliest of these was the famous monastery founded by Columcille at Iona in western Scotland from which he and his companions and successors worked among the Scottish Picts. The greatest of the Irish missionaries was Columbanus, a man of great vitality and wide learning who founded monasteries in Luxeuil and other places in France and at Bobbio in northern Italy, where he died.

This cultural flowering at home and its expansion abroad at a time when Ireland itself was comparatively peaceful led future generations to look back upon the period from the sixth to the ninth centuries as Ireland's Golden Age.

By the ninth century, Irish monasteries had grown in wealth and importance and attracted the attentions of Norse freebooters. Later in the century, Viking settlements, both Norse and Danish, along the coast provided the nucleus of the later cities of Dublin, Limerick and Waterford, each forming a separate kingdom frequently at war with neighbouring Irish kings though sometimes in alliance with them against others.

A second wave of Viking attacks in the early and mid-tenth century consolidated these settlements and led to more extensive penetration of the island and disruption of the existing order. The Vikings established a lasting urban, trading and shipping tradition and issued the first Irish coins.

The Uí Néill of Tara with ramifications in Ulster had early achieved a position of dominance in the north of the country while the Kings of Munster achieved a similar position in the south, both competing for control of Leinster. During the Viking period, war

27

History

37. *Detail from* The Marriage of Strongbow and Eva *by the 19th-century Irish painter, Daniel Maclise.* Strongbow, the *leader of the Norman invaders, married Dermot MacMurrough's daughter.*

between the various Irish kings gradually took the form of a struggle for control of the whole island.

The Munster king, Brian Ború, first made the High Kingship of Ireland a universally accepted reality in 1002 but died fighting against a rebellious Leinster aided by the Norse in the battle of Clontarf (1014). He did not, however, succeed in establishing a permanent dynasty and, for a century and a half after his death, the High Kingship was contested in a struggle which ended with the victory of the Connacht dynasty of O'Connor.

By the twelfth century, Ireland was moving towards feudal structures. At the same time, the work of men such as St Malachy and St Laurence O'Toole had reformed the Church and brought about the adoption of the Continental model with dioceses, in most cases co-terminous with the political divisions of the day.

In 1166, the Leinster king, Dermot MacMurrough, lost his kingdom and sought the aid of Henry II of England to regain it. A small force of Norman adventurers came to his assistance in 1169 and soon established themselves in large areas of the country. Henry claimed suzerainty over Ireland and came in person in 1172. His claims were recognised by the Church and by many Irish kings.

Henry's preoccupations and those of his successors with affairs in France left the field in Ireland largely to the Norman settlers who over the centuries were to a large extent assimilated to the Gaelic order. Central authority over the Anglo-Norman colony was progressively eroded until by the 15th century only a small area around Dublin (known as the Pale) was effectively under English rule.

Under the Tudor rulers, Henry VIII, Mary and Elizabeth, the authority of the English crown was asserted throughout Ireland, leading to the final defeat of the traditional Gaelic-Irish leaders, Hugh O'Neill and Hugh O'Donnell, at Kinsale in 1601.

History

The lands of these and other leaders in north-west Ireland were confiscated and settled in 1609 with large numbers of Protestant English and Scottish colonists who differed in language and religion from the native Irish who had remained Roman Catholic at the Reformation. Largely because of the religious difference, these settlers did not assimilate with the native population as earlier settlers had done.

The differences between the English government and the Catholic Irish, native and colonists alike, were accentuated by a rebellion in 1641-50 which was ruthlessly crushed by Oliver Cromwell, after which the ownership of land in Ireland was placed almost entirely in Protestant hands.

The victory of William of Orange in 1690 confirmed this arrangement which was further protected for over a century by a series of laws discriminating against the Catholic and Dissenter population. These penal laws reduced consciousness of social class among the Catholics while heightening their sense of national origin. They also had the effect of encouraging many Catholics and Dissenters to emigrate to the American colonies where their descendants played a large part in the American Revolution.

Towards the end of the 18th century, the Protestant ascendancy that had thus been established felt sufficiently strong to relax many of the disabilities under which Catholics suffered. At the same time, under leaders such as Henry Flood and Henry Grattan, the Irish Parliament (which represented only the Anglican ascendancy) succeeded in obtaining almost complete legislative independence from Britain in 1782 but lost it in 1800 after the failure of a series of rebellions.

The main rebellion included Irishmen of all religions and was planned by the United Irishmen, a society which had been founded by Theobald Wolfe Tone in 1791 under the influence of the American and French Revolutions with the object of uniting Catholic,

History

41. Irish emigrants leaving Queenstown (now Cobh) Harbour, an engraving from the Illustrated London News *of September 1874.*

Protestant and Dissenter in order to 'break the connection with England'.

The Act of Union of 1800 abolished the Irish Parliament and made Ireland part of the United Kingdom. The penal laws were largely repealed by 1793 and the final disability was removed in 1829 when Daniel O'Connell secured entry to Parliament at Westminster for Catholics.

The population increased very rapidly in the first half of the 19th century to reach 8 ½ million by 1841. The mass of the people, however, were landless tenants dependent for survival on the potato and, when it failed in most of the years between 1846 and 1851, up to a million are thought to have died of starvation and disease and a further million emigrated, mainly to America. Emigration continued at a high level throughout the century following the famine with the result that by 1961 the population had fallen by half.

A further consequence of the famine was the rapid spread of the English language throughout the country as parents encouraged their children to learn English in order to facilitate their assimilation in the countries to which they would have to emigrate. Once the tradition of mass emigration had begun, there was a rapid transition to English over increasing areas of the country. The process was aided by the provision of free primary education through the medium of English in national schools which had been introduced in 1831.

After the achievement of Catholic Emancipation, Daniel O'Connell had turned his attention to creating a mass movement with the object of bringing about by constitutional means a repeal of the Act of Union of 1800. He did not achieve this objective, in part at least because of the poverty of his Catholic supporters whose representation in Parliament was limited by property franchise restrictions that were not relaxed until much later in the century.

History

Despite the Act of Union and the failure of the Repeal movement, the sense of Irish nationhood remained strong. In the late 1840s, a group known as the Young Ireland movement which included Protestant leaders such as William Smith O'Brien, John Mitchel and Thomas Davis developed the ideals of the United Irishmen and, inspired by a series of nationalist revolts in Europe in that year, attempted a rebellion in 1848.

In 1856, the Irish Republican Brotherhood (also known as the Fenians) was founded in Ireland and the United States by veterans of the 1848 rebellion. The IRB was a secret oath-bound society convinced that independence could only be achieved through armed revolution.

This movement owed much to the Irish emigrants in the United States who began at this time to emerge as a significant factor in Irish history. The Irish in America were by now politically well organised, financially prosperous relative to the Irish at home, and willing to support any movement for Irish independence. Despite the failure of an attempted rising in 1867, the IRB survived into the 20th century and played a large part in the Easter Rising of 1916.

After the apparent failure of Fenianism in the 1860s, political activity increased, at first directed towards bettering the lot of the great number of tenant farmers whose position had not been improved by the reduction in population after the Famine because they were subject to exorbitant rents and remained always under the threat of eviction.

The campaign for land reform was begun by Michael Davitt, a former Fenian, who founded the Land League in 1879. The League developed into a mass movement and was strongly supported in Parliament by Irish political leaders. It received considerable financial assistance from the American Irish. The League's activities resulted in a number of land reforms which gradually eliminated the worst agrarian abuses. Finally, in 1903, Wyndham's Act effectively

History

transferred ownership of the land to the farmers who worked it.

The campaign for land reform had received powerful support in Parliament from a new generation of political leaders. Chief among these was Charles Stewart Parnell (1846-91) who came into prominence during the Land War of 1879-82 and was by 1885 the undisputed leader of the Irish people. His Irish Parliamentary Party held over 80% of all Irish seats at Westminster and at times controlled the balance of power there. During the period of Parnell's leadership, the first Home Rule Bill was introduced in the House of Commons but was defeated in the House of Lords.

In Ireland the movement for Home Rule was strongly resisted by most Protestants and especially by the numerically important Protestant section of the community in the northern counties. The 19th century had brought increasing prosperity to the north-east of Ireland and Belfast had become the leading centre of industry on the island. Protestants generally felt that the Union worked to their advantage and had little sympathy with the Home Rule movement which, if successful, would have placed them in a minority in a self-governing and overwhelmingly Roman Catholic Ireland.

When a third Home Rule Bill passed the Commons in 1912, Sir Edward Carson, supported by the British Conservative and Unionist Party and with arms secured in Germany, established a military organisation, the Ulster Volunteer Force, to resist Home Rule by force, if necessary.

In 1913, the Irish Volunteers were founded as a direct counter to the establishment of the Ulster Volunteer Force. The British Government proved to be unwilling to deal with Unionist resistance to Home Rule and, when the Home Rule Bill was eventually placed on the statute book in 1914, it contained a provision which enabled the supporters of Carson to opt out of the

43. Grand reception of James Stephens, the Fenian chief, at Jones' Wood, April 15, 1866 from Harper's Weekly.

44. Charles Stewart Parnell *painted by SP Hall.*

45. Charles Kickham, novelist and editor of the Fenian paper, The Irish People.

History

46. Cúchulainn, mythological hero of the Irish preChristian sagas, is depicted in the memorial to the 1916 Rising in the General Post Office, Dublin, which was the headquarters of the Rising.

scope of its provisions for a period: The operation of this limited Bill was suspended for the duration of the First World War and many members of the Irish Volunteers, on the advice of John Redmond, leader of the Irish Parliamentary Party, joined the British Army in the war.

However, a large section of the Irish Volunteer Movement under the leadership of Pádraic Pearse and the trade union Citizen Army under the leadership of James Connolly organised an armed rising which took place on Easter Monday, 1916. Pearse proclaimed the Irish Republic as a sovereign state and with about 1,000 men, the Volunteers and the Citizen Army held part of Dublin for a week against British Forces.

The execution of the leaders of the 1916 Rising after their surrender aroused support throughout the country for their objectives. This support was shown at the general election of 1918, which produced a massive swing of public opinion away from the Irish Parliamentary Party to the Independence Party, *Sinn Féin*, which gained 73 of the 105 Parliamentary seats.

The *Sinn Féin* members, ignoring the British Parliament, met in Dublin on 21 January 1919, issued a declaration confirming the Republic proclaimed in 1916 and constituted themselves the National Parliament *(Dáil)*. A Provisional Government was appointed under the Presidency of Éamon de Valera. The efforts of the British Government to suppress the *Dáil* and the Irish Volunteers led to the War of Independence. The Provisional Government's military operations were under the direction of Cathal Brugha and Michael Collins.

In 1920, the British Parliament passed the Government of Ireland Act which effectively imposed two separate Home Rule systems of government on Ireland and led in 1921 to the establishment of a Parliament for the six north-eastern counties of Antrim, Armagh, Derry, Down, Fermanagh and Tyrone.

"WE DECLARE, THE RIGHT OF THE PEOPLE OF IRELAND TO THE OWNERSHIP OF IRELAND, AND TO THE UNFETTERED CONTROL OF IRISH DESTINIES, TO BE SOVEREIGN AND INDEFEASIBLE. THE LONG USURPATION OF THAT RIGHT BY A FOREIGN PEOPLE AND GOVERNMENT HAS NOT EXTINGUISHED THE RIGHT, NOR CAN IT EVER BE EXTINGUISHED EXCEPT BY THE DESTRUCTION OF THE IRISH PEOPLE. IN EVERY GENERATION THE IRISH PEOPLE HAVE ASSERTED THEIR RIGHT TO NATIONAL FREEDOM AND SOVEREIGNTY: SIX TIMES DURING THE PAST THREE HUNDRED YEARS THEY HAVE ASSERTED IT IN ARMS. STANDING ON THAT FUNDAMENTAL RIGHT AND AGAIN ASSERTING IT IN ARMS IN THE FACE OF THE WORLD, WE HEREBY PROCLAIM THE IRISH REPUBLIC AS A SOVEREIGN INDEPENDENT STATE, AND WE PLEDGE OUR LIVES AND THE LIVES OF OUR COMRADES IN ARMS TO THE CAUSE OF ITS FREEDOM, OF ITS WELFARE, AND OF ITS EXALTATION AMONG THE NATIONS."

THOMAS J. CLARKE.

SEAN MacDIARMADA,   THOMAS MacDONAGH,
P.H PEARSE,   EAMONN CEANNT,
JAMES CONNOLLY.   JOSEPH PLUNKETT.

47. Arthur Griffith
painted by Sir John
Lavery.

48. Michael Collins
painted by Sarah
Harrison.

49. Éamon de Valera
addressing an
election rally in
Kilkenny, 1917.

50. Edward Carson
signing the Ulster
Covenant, a solemn
promise to resist
Home Rule in 1912.
On his left is Sir
James Craig, later
Prime Minister of
Northern Ireland.

History

On 11 July 1921, a truce was declared in the War of Independence and peace negotiations were opened between the Irish and British Governments. On 6 December 1921, the Articles of Agreement for a Treaty between Ireland and Great Britain were signed in London. The Treaty provided for the establishment of an Irish Free State as a Dominion of the British Commonwealth but allowed the Parliament in Belfast to decide whether the six counties which it represented should opt to stay with Britain, an option which they immediately exercised.

The Treaty provisions were accepted by 64 votes to 57 in *Dáil Éireann.* The Civil War which followed ended in May 1923 in the defeat of those who wished to maintain the Republic and were opposed to the Treaty. This war claimed the lives of Michael Collins and of Cathal Brugha.

The Irish State

History

After the deaths of Arthur Griffith and Michael Collins
in August 1922, the Government of the Irish Free
State was led by WT Cosgrave, head of the *Cumann
na nGaedheal* Party. A Constitution for the new State
was adopted in December 1922 and, in 1925, the
Government accepted the existing border between
Northern Ireland and the Free State when it became
clear that the Boundary Commission had not
recommended the expected changes.

In 1926, Éamon de Valera, who as President of the
Republic had opposed the Treaty, founded the
Fianna Fáil Party. *Fianna Fáil* came to power after the
1932 election, with support from minority groups,
and proceeded to abolish the oath of allegiance to
the British Crown and other restrictive clauses of the
Treaty of 1921. An 'economic war' followed in
June 1932 when the British Government imposed a
tax of 40% on Irish exports to Britain in retaliation
for the retention by Ireland of the Irish land annuities.
A new constitution declaring Ireland to be 'a
sovereign, independent, democratic state' was
adopted in a referendum in 1937. In 1938, by
agreement, Britain relinquished the naval facilities
which it held under the Treaty and brought the
'economic war' to an end. When the Second World
War broke out, Ireland declared its neutrality.

Fianna Fáil remained in power until 1948 when a
Coalition Government of members of the *Fine Gael*,
Labour and other parties led by John A Costello took
office. This Coalition Government in 1949 repealed
the External Relations Act (1936) and provided that
the 'description of the State shall be the Republic of
Ireland', a step which led to Ireland leaving the
Commonwealth.

Following the general election of 1951, *Fianna Fáil*
were returned to power until 1954 when the
Coalition regained office for a period of three years. In
the period from 1948 to 1957, steps were taken by
both the Coalition and *Fianna Fáil* Governments to
orientate the protected Irish manufacturing sectors

51
52

53
54

55
56

Since its establishment under the 1937 Constitution, the office of President of Ireland has been held by:

51. Douglas Hyde (1938-45)

52. Seán T Ó Ceallaigh (1945-59)

53. Éamon de Valera (1959-73)

54. Erskine H Childers (1973-74)

55. Cearbhall Ó Dálaigh (1974-76)

56. Patrick J Hillery (1976-)

The Heads of
Government of
Ireland to date have
been:

57. W T Cosgrave
(1922-32)

Éamon de Valera
(1932-48, 1951-
54, 1957-59) see
53 across

58. John A Costello
(1948-51, 1954-
57)

59. Seán F Lemass
(1959-66)

60. Liam Cosgrave
(1973-77)

61. John M Lynch
(1966-73, 1977-
79)

61a. Charles J
Haughey (1979-81)

62. Garret FitzGerald
(1981-   )

57

58
59

60
61

61a
62

History

towards external markets and to expand the industrial base of the country. In the general election of 1957, *Fianna Fáil* were returned to power and were re-elected in successive elections up to 1973. A substantially faster economic growth was generated resulting in the achievement of a growth rate of about 4% during the 1960s and in the elimination by the early '70s of net emigration which had reached exceptional levels in the mid-1950s.

In 1959, Éamon de Valera, having relinquished the leadership of *Fianna Fáil*, was elected President of Ireland. He was succeeded as *Taoiseach* (Prime Minister) by Seán F Lemass (1959-66) who in turn was succeeded by John M Lynch who was Taoiseach from 1966 to 1973.

In 1972, Ireland decided to join the European Economic Community in a referendum in which 83% of the votes were cast in favour of membership. In the general election of 1973, a Coalition of the *Fine Gael* and Labour parties was elected. This Government under the leadership of Liam T Cosgrave was defeated in the general election of 1977 when Mr Lynch returned as *Taoiseach*. In 1979, Mr Lynch resigned as *Taoiseach* and he was succeeded by Charles J Haughey. Following the general election of 1981, a Coalition Government of the *Fine Gael* and Labour parties again came to power, with Dr Garret FitzGerald as *Taoiseach*.

63. Nigerian students under instruction at the Poolbeg station in Dublin, an example of the ESB's thriving foreign consultancy work.

64. Dr Patrick J Hillery, then Minister for Foreign Affairs, and Mr John M Lynch, Prime Minister, signing the Treaty of Accession to the EEC in January 1972.

Constitution

The basic law of the State is the Constitution of Ireland adopted by referendum in 1937. The Constitution sets out the form of government and defines the powers of the President and Parliament (the *Oireachtas*) and of the Government. It also defines the structure and powers of the Courts, sets out the fundamental rights of citizens and contains a number of directive principles of social policy for the general guidance of the *Oireachtas*.

The Constitution may be amended only as a result of a Bill passed by the *Oireachtas* and subsequently approved in a referendum. Up to mid-1978, six such Bills had been passed by the *Oireachtas* of which three were subsequently approved by referendum.

Any citizen has the right to petition the Courts to secure his rights under the Constitution or to have a judgement pronounced as to whether given legislation is compatible with the Constitution. Moreover, the President may before signing a Bill refer it to the Supreme Court for a decision on its compatibility with the Constitution. These procedures have been employed on a number of occasions and the Courts have from time to time declared a number of laws or parts of laws to be unconstitutional and consequently void.

Flag and Emblem

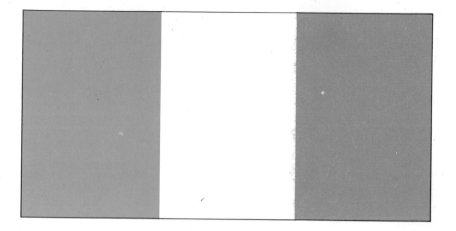

National Anthem

Sin — ne Fian — na Fáil, a — tá faoi gheall ag Éi — rinn, Buíon dár
Sol — diers are we, whose lives are pledged to Ire — land; Some have

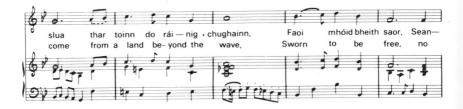

slua thar toinn do rái — nig chughainn, Faoi mhóid bheith saor, Sean—
come from a land be- yond the wave, Sworn to be free, no

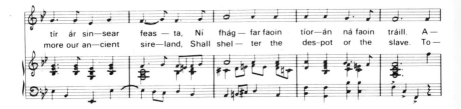

tír ár sin—sear feas — ta, Ní fhág — far faoin tíor — án ná faoin tráill. A —
more our an—cient sire—land, Shall shel — ter the des-pot or the slave. To—

nocht a théam sa bhear—na baoil, Le gean ar Ghaeil chun báis nó saoil, Le
night we man the *"bear-na baoil",* In Er — in's cause, come woe or weal, 'Mid

gun—na scréach, faoi lámhach na bpi — léar, Seo libh canaíg amh-rán na bhFiann.
can—non's roar and ri — fles peal, We'll chant a sol—dier's song.

Rit.

(*gap of danger)

52

Government

Form of Government

Ireland is a parliamentary democracy. It has two Houses of Parliament, an elected President who is Head of State and a Prime Minister *(Taoiseach)* who is Head of Government.

The President

The President of Ireland *(Uachtarán na hÉireann)* is elected by direct vote of the people for not more than two terms, each of seven years. He normally acts on the advice and authority of the Government but performs some of his functions in consultation with an advisory Council of State. He signs and promulgates Bills passed by Parliament and receives and accredits ambassadors. As guardian of the Constitution he may on occasion submit a Bill passed by Parliament to the people in a referendum or refer it to the Supreme Court to decide whether it contravenes the Constitution. On the advice of the Taoiseach, the President summons and dissolves Parliament but may refuse to dissolve Parliament on the advice of a *Taoiseach* who has ceased to retain the support of a majority in the *Dáil*. Subject to the law, the supreme command of the Armed Forces is vested in the President.

The Legislature

The National Parliament *(Oireachtas)* consists of the President and two Houses — a House of Representatives *(Dáil Éireann)* and a Senate *(Seanad Éireann)*. All laws passed by the *Oireachtas* must conform to the Constitution.

Dáil Éireann

Members of the *Dáil*, who are known as *Teachtaí Dála* (usually abbreviated to TD), are elected by adult suffrage in secret ballot under a system of proportional representation. An election is held at least every five years. Each constituency elects from 3 to 5 members, depending on population. At present there are 166 TDs elected from 41 constituencies.

65. Pictured above with President Hillery are members of the Government and the
Attorney General who took office on 30 June 1981:

Front row, (from left to right):

Minister for Defence
James Tully, TD

Taoiseach (Prime Minister)
Garret fitzGerald, TD

President Hillery

Tánaiste (Deputy Prime Minister) and
Minister for Industry and Energy
Michael O'Leary, TD

Minister for the Environment
Peter Barry, TD

Minister for Health and for Social Welfare
Eileen Desmond, TD

Attorney General
Peter Sutherland

Back row, (from left to right):

Minister for Finance
John Bruton, TD

Minister for Fisheries and Forestry
Tom Fitzpatrick, TD

Minister for Labour and for the Public
Service
Liam Kavanagh, TD

Minister for Agriculture
Alan Dukes, TD

Minister for Justice
Jim Mitchell, TD

Minister for Transport and for Posts and
Telegraphs
Patrick Cooney, TD

Minister for Trade, Commerce and
Tourism
John Kelly, TD

Minister for Education
John Boland, TD

Minister for the Gaeltacht
Paddy O'Toole, TD

Minister for Foreign Affairs
Senator James Dooge

Dáil Éireann

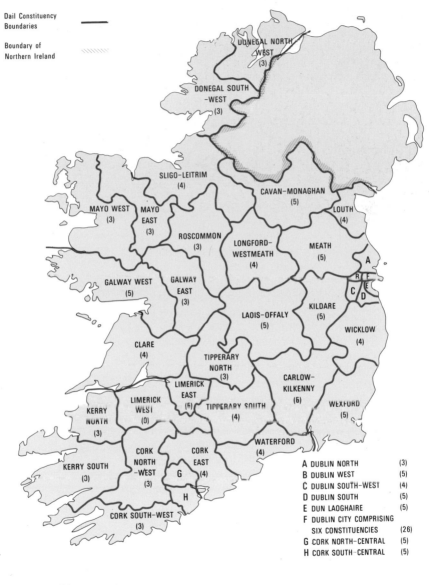

Dail Constituency Boundaries

Boundary of Northern Ireland

DONEGAL NORTH WEST (3)

DONEGAL SOUTH -WEST (3)

SLIGO-LEITRIM (4)

CAVAN-MONAGHAN (5)

MAYO WEST (3)

MAYO EAST (3)

ROSCOMMON (3)

LONGFORD-WESTMEATH (4)

MEATH (5)

LOUTH (4)

A

GALWAY WEST (5)

GALWAY EAST (3)

LAOIS-OFFALY (5)

KILDARE (5)

WICKLOW (4)

CLARE (4)

TIPPERARY NORTH (3)

CARLOW-KILKENNY (6)

LIMERICK EAST (5)

LIMERICK WEST (0)

TIPPERARY SOUTH (4)

WEXFORD (5)

KERRY NORTH (3)

WATERFORD (4)

CORK NORTH -WEST (3)

CORK EAST (4)

KERRY SOUTH (3)

G

H

CORK SOUTH-WEST (3)

A DUBLIN NORTH (3)
B DUBLIN WEST (5)
C DUBLIN SOUTH-WEST (4)
D DUBLIN SOUTH (5)
E DUN LAOGHAIRE (5)
F DUBLIN CITY COMPRISING
  SIX CONSTITUENCIES (26)
G CORK NORTH-CENTRAL (5)
H CORK SOUTH-CENTRAL (5)

Scale 1:3,000,000

30 20 10 0   30   60 Km

30   20   10   0   30 Miles

Prepared at the Ordnance Survey Dublin

© Government of Ireland 1981

55

Government

Seanad Éireann

The Senate *(Seanad Éireann)* has sixty members, eleven nominated by the Head of Government, forty-three elected to represent various vocational and cultural interests and six elected by the universities. The Senate may initiate a Bill other than a Money Bill. It may delay a Bill passed by the *Dáil* for a maximum of ninety days or it may suggest changes in the Bill, but it cannot block it permanently.

The Government

The executive power of the people is exercised by the Government or on its authority. Under the Constitution, the Government must consist of not less than seven or more than fifteen members. It acts as a collective authority responsible to the *Dáil*. The *Taoiseach* is appointed by the President on the nomination of the *Dáil*. He must resign when the Government which he leads, whether it is a minority or majority Government, ceases to retain majority support in the *Dáil*. In practice, following a general election, the prospective *Taoiseach* first secures the support of a majority in the new *Dáil* and then receives his formal appointment from the President.

The Civil Service

The administration and business of the public services of the State are at present divided between eighteen Government Departments: the Departments of the *Taoiseach*; Agriculture; Defence; Education; Environment; Finance; Fisheries and Forestry; Foreign Affairs; Gaeltacht; Health; Industry and Energy; Justice; Labour; Posts and Telegraphs; Public Service; Social Welfare; Trade, Commerce and Tourism and Transport. Each Department is headed by a Government Minister. As the maximum number of Government Ministers under the Constitution is fifteen, three members of the Government currently hold two portfolios each: one member acts as Minister for Labour and Minister for the Public Service, one acts as Minister for Health and Minister for Social Welfare and one as Minister for Transport and Minister for Posts and Telegraphs.

European Parliament

European Parliament
Constituency Boundaries

Boundary of
Northern Ireland

CONNACHT – ULSTER (3)

NORTHERN IRELAND
(3)

DUBLIN
(4)

LEINSTER
(3)

MUNSTER
(5)

Scale 1:3,000,000

30 20 10   0   30   60 Km

30   20   10   0   30 Miles

Prepared at the Ordnance Survey Dublin

© Government of Ireland 1978

66

67

66. The chamber of Seanad Éireann.

67. The chamber of Dáil Éireann.

68. St Patrick's Hall, Dublin Castle, the most impressive of the State Apartments. The Apartments are used for the most important State receptions. Formerly the ceremonial meetings of the Order of Knights of St Patrick took place in the Hall and stallplates, crests, helmets and banners of some of the Knights adorn the walls.

69. George's Hall, Dublin Castle, also in the State Apartments, built as a supper room for the visit of King George V of England in 1911. A noteworthy feature of the room is the paintings by the 18th-century Flemish artist, Peter de Gree.

Government

*Below, the symbols
of Kilkenny Design
Workshops*

In addition to the Departments, many offices
attached to Departments discharge a variety of
specific functions. Amongst the largest of these are
the Office of the Revenue Commissioners and the
Office of Public Works.

The headquarters of all Departments are located in
Dublin, but many Departments have local offices
throughout the country. Recruitment to posts in the
Civil Service is by means of open competition run by
the Civil Service Commission and selection is on
merit. The Civil Service is the country's largest single
employer, employing about 54,000 people.

State-sponsored bodies

A group of almost one hundred bodies, known as
State-sponsored bodies, carries out a wide range of
specific tasks on behalf of the Government.

*and the National Film
Studios respectively.*

These bodies are generally divided into two groups.
The 'commercial' group includes those bodies which
are engaged in trading or commercial operations,
while the 'non-commercial' group includes those
which are promotional or regulatory or which are
involved in research.

Within general policy guidelines laid down by the
Government, State-sponsored bodies have a
significant amount of autonomy. Although the
Government or an individual Minister usually appoints
members to the Boards or Councils of the bodies,
they are not subject to detailed Ministerial control
over day-to-day matters.

Some State-sponsored bodies have been created by
a State take-over of existing enterprises (e.g. *Córas
Iompair Éireann* — The National Transport System).
Many more have been established to supplement
private enterprise in the financial or industrial sectors
or in the area of infrastructural development. Several
were established to regulate a profession or trade.

The organisational form and the method of their

*70. The Kilkenny
Shop, Dublin, is
operated by Kilkenny
Design Workshops,
a State-sponsored
body established by
the Government to
improve design in
industry and provide
a showplace for
good design.*

*71. The National
Film Studios of
Ireland on location at
Adare Manor, Adare,
Co. Limerick: Marty
Feldman and Michael
York prepare for a
fencing scene in* The
Last Remake of Beau
Geste. *The National
Film Studios were
established by the
Government in
1975.*

Government

72. This sculpture by Oisín Kelly, one of the most distinguished of modern Irish sculptors, is outside Cork County Hall.

financing differ widely between the various bodies. Some are statutory corporations while others are public or even private companies established under the Companies Acts.

State-sponsored bodies, which together employ a total of about 65,700 people, play a vital role in the economic and social life of the country.

Local Government

Elected local authorities (county councils, county boroughs, boroughs, urban district councils and town commissioners) are responsible for local administration in Ireland. Their administration of the laws dealing with local government is supervised by the Department of the Environment. There are 115 local authorities of varying size with responsibility for a range of services, including housing and building, road transportation and safety, water supply and sewerage, development incentives and controls, environmental protection, recreational amenities, agriculture, education, health and welfare and miscellaneous services. Major policy decisions are taken by the members of each local authority, who are elected by adult suffrage at regular intervals. Day-to-day administration is conducted by permanent officials under a city or county manager.

The expenditure of local authorities is met in part from State grants and other receipts such as rents and charges and in part from the proceeds of a 'rate' or property tax levied yearly by each major local authority on immovable property, other than residential property, in its area. Town commissioners are not rating authorities and their requirements, apart from State grants and miscellaneous receipts, are obtained from the county council for the area. In 1979, total capital expenditure on local government in Ireland was estimated at approximately IR£205 million, while current expenditure was estimated at IR£437 million.

Legal System

In the earliest times the system of law prevailing in Ireland was known as Brehon Law. With the progressive extension to the whole country of English rule, the Brehon Laws gradually disappeared and, by the beginning of the 17th century, justice was being administered according to English legal concepts and common law. Modern Irish law is based on English common law as modified by subsequent legislation and the Constitution of 1937.

Judges are appointed from senior practising members of the legal profession. They are guaranteed independence in the exercise of their functions and may be removed from office only for misbehaviour or incapacity by resolution of both Houses of Parliament.

The High Court has the power to determine all matters of law and fact, civil and criminal, including the validity of any legislation, having regard to the provisions of the Constitution (except legislation which has already been referred to the Supreme Court by the President of Ireland). When hearing criminal cases it is called the Central Criminal Court. In all criminal cases and most civil cases, the Court consists of a judge sitting with a jury of twelve ordinary citizens, who determine all issues of fact and assess damages in civil cases. The judge decides on the sentence in criminal cases within the limits imposed by the law.

There are courts of limited jurisdiction which hear cases of lesser magnitude. These courts sit locally whereas the High Court usually sits in Dublin. The Circuit Court has jurisdiction to hear all the main criminal offences except murder, treason, piracy and allied offences. The judge sits with a jury, as in the High Court. In civil cases there is no jury and the court's jurisdiction is usually limited to claims not exceeding IR£2,000.

The District Court consists of a judge called a district justice who has a civil jurisdiction limited to claims of

Legal System

IR£250 and hears summary offences. He sits without a jury and in general may not sentence an offender to more than twelve months' imprisonment, a fine of IR£500, or both.

There is an elaborate system of appeals. Decisions of the District Court may be appealed to the Circuit Court. Decisions of the Circuit Court in civil cases may be appealed to the High Court. Verdicts of the Circuit Court and the Central Criminal Court in criminal cases may be appealed to the Court of Criminal Appeal, a court which consists of three judges drawn from the High Court and the Supreme Court.

The Supreme Court is the Court of Final Appeal. It hears appeals from the High Court or the Court of Criminal Appeal and, on questions of law, it hears cases referred from the Circuit Court. The Supreme Court consists of the Chief Justice and five ordinary judges. The president of the High Court is, *ex officio*, an additional judge of the Supreme Court.

There is legislation providing for the establishment of Special Criminal Courts whenever the Government is satisfied that the ordinary Courts are inadequate to secure the effective administration of justice and the preservation of public peace and order. There is no jury in cases heard before these Courts but, in most other respects, procedure governing them is the same as in criminal trials generally. A Special Criminal Court consisting of both serving and retired members of the judiciary has been in existence since 1972.

Although there is a limited right of private prosecution, most prosecutions are instituted by the Director of Public Prosecutions on behalf of the State. The Director is a civil servant and is independent in the performance of his functions. In civil proceedings the State is represented by the Attorney General who is, under the Constitution, adviser to the Government in matters of law and legal opinion. The Attorney General is not a member of the Government, but his tenure of office is co-terminous with that of the Government.

Legal System

73. The Four Courts, Dublin, where the superior courts of Ireland are located. They are the work of the great 18th-century architect, James Gandon, who was also responsible for some of the other outstanding public buildings of the classical period in Dublin.

The legal profession is divided into barristers and solicitors. Barristers generally specialise in the presentation of cases in court and may be retained only on the instructions of a solicitor. Solicitors seldom conduct cases personally other than in the District Court. In addition to litigation they deal with legal business of a sort that rarely goes to court e.g. the transfer of houses and the administration of the assets of deceased persons. While all barristers practise individually, solicitors frequently practise in partnership with one another.

The Honourable Society of King's Inns (founded in 1541) is the body with responsibility for the training of barristers. The Incorporated Law Society (founded in 1852) has a similar function in respect of solicitors. Both societies conduct courses in the professional or technical aspects of law but rely mainly on the university law faculties for courses in academic law subjects.

Police

The Irish police force, *An Garda Síochána*, was
established in 1922. It is the sole police force in the
State and is unarmed. It is a centralised agency
under the direction of the Minister for Justice. At its
head is the Commissioner, who is appointed by the
Government. The command structure is composed of
Deputy Commissioners, Assistant Commissioners,
Chief Superintendents, Superintendents, Inspectors
and Sergeants. Entry to the force is at the rank of
Garda (the basic grade officer). The force of 10,000
operates in 23 divisions, each divided into districts
and sub-districts. It includes regular and special forces
for crime detection and prevention, and carries out
local administrative functions as well.

Among developed countries, Ireland has one of the
lowest incidences of serious crimes of violence while
the crime detection rate is comparable to that of other
countries.

Among the more challenging areas of *Garda* activity
in recent years has been the problem of rapid
urbanisation, while effective policing of a circuitous
border with Northern Ireland in co-operation with the
Defence Forces since 1969 has absorbed a
considerable section of the Force's resources.

Prisons

There are nine prisons and places of detention in
Ireland under the control of the Department of
Justice. These include closed secure prisons, open
centres and an industrial training centre which provide
a wide range of services and activities aimed at
helping the offender to improve his capability of living
usefully in the community after his release.

At any time there are about 1,200 persons in
custody and over 1,600 persons on probation, under
supervision or on parole to the Welfare Service of the
Department of Justice.

Gabh le hArm an Lae Inniu.

An tEolas go léir le fáil ón bPost Arm is gaire duit nó ó Cheannceathrú an F.C.A.

Defence

The total strength of the Defence Forces stood at
33,000 in April 1980 and accounted for an
estimated expenditure of IR£144 million, or 4.8% of
total Government expenditure for the year. The
strength of the Permanent Defence Force, which
includes the regular Army, the Air Corps and the
Naval Service is 16,200. The reserve Defence force,
comprising the First Line Reserve, *An Fórsa Cosanta
Áitiúil* (Second Line Army Reserve) and *An Slua Muirí*
(Second Line Naval Reserve) has a strength of
16,800.

All recruitment to the Defence Forces is on a
voluntary basis with a minimum enlistment in the
Permanent Defence Force and the First Line Reserve
of three years (four for the Naval Service and three
for the First Line Naval Reserve). Officers are
normally recruited through the medium of cadetships
and undergo an 18-month course of training before
appointment.

Under the Constitution, supreme command of the
Forces is vested in the President, but military
command is exercised by the Government through
the Minister for Defence. The Minister is aided and
advised on matters relating to his Department by a
Council of Defence, consisting of two civilian and
three military members. For purposes of
administration the country is divided into four
territorial military commands — the Eastern,
Southern, Western and Curragh Commands. Each of
the four Brigades in the Army consists of two
infantry battalions and a squadron or company from
each Corps (except Ordnance and Air).

There are, in addition, special military establishments
which include a Military College, an Army Equitation
School, an Army School of Music and an Army
Apprentice School. The Army Equitation School
provides all cadets with an equestrian course. The
participation of Army teams at international shows
and gymkhanas also demonstrates the worth of the
Irish horse at home and abroad.

Defence

The Naval Service has three coastal minesweepers, four fishery patrol vessels and a supply training vessel. Plans are at an advanced stage for the design of two further patrol vessels which will be capable of carrying helicopters. The equipment of the Air Corps comprises 37 aircraft, including helicopters which, as well as playing an important rôle in security operations, provide rescue, ambulance and other services.

Ireland is not a member of a military alliance. However, since 1958, Irish troops have formed part of many United Nations peace-keeping missions. They have seen service in the Middle East, Congo (now Zaire), Cyprus, West New Guinea (now West Irian), India, Pakistan and Lebanon.

Primary responsibility for internal security rests with the police *(Garda Síochána)*. The Defence Forces, pursuant to their rôle of rendering aid to the civil power, assist the *Garda Síochána* as required, for example, in patrolling and checkpoint duties, guarding prisons and installations of national importance and in bomb disposal operations.

Northern Ireland

*Having opted to remain outside the provisions of the
Anglo-Irish Treaty of 1921, Northern Ireland has
since then been separately administered as a part of
the United Kingdom of Great Britain and Northern
Ireland. In the following pages some general
information regarding the history and administration
of Northern Ireland is given. More detailed
information may be found in the sources given in the
bibliography on page 248.*

History

Political activity in Northern Ireland since the establishment of a Parliament in Belfast has broadly reflected the division between nationalist and unionist traditions. Although Britain periodically reaffirmed the status of Northern Ireland as part of the United Kingdom, successive British Governments took little direct interest in the internal affairs of the area up to the late 1960s. The general policies of Northern Ireland governments were designed to secure a level of British financial contributions to enable the Northern Ireland government services to maintain parity with British services. Government until 1972 remained firmly in the hands of the ruling Unionist Party with the minority representatives in opposition. Intermittent violence flared up with varying degrees of intensity in every decade since 1920.

In the late 1960s, a civil rights movement in Northern Ireland succeeded in achieving some of the more obvious reforms sought by the minority, but in their activities, civil rights leaders also attracted considerable resistance and hostility from some Unionists. Despite the reforms, the basic problem remained in that the minority was still completely excluded from any voice in the government of Northern Ireland.

Extremist Protestants attacked civil rights meetings and Catholic homes on a wide scale in 1969. The Government of Northern Ireland responded under pressure from Britain by committing the British Army to maintain peace. Although initially welcomed by Catholics, the Army was gradually felt by the minority to be a further instrument of the Government of Northern Ireland under whose control it acted. This situation was exploited by the paramilitary Provisional IRA which commenced a campaign of violence against the security forces in Northern Ireland. Protestant paramilitary groups also began to engage in acts of violence. By 1980 violence in the North had claimed over 2,000 lives.

The alienation of the minority community led

History

76. Detail of the painting, The Twelfth of July in Portadown by Sir John Lavery, one of the outstanding Irish artists in the early years of this century. The painting depicts a parade of the Orange Order. Each year on 12 July these colourful parades take place to commemorate the victory of William of Orange over James II at the Battle of the Boyne in 1690.

ultimately to the suspension of the Northern Ireland Parliament in March 1972 and its replacement by direct rule from the British Parliament at Westminster.

Following a conference held at Sunningdale in December 1973 attended by representatives of the British and Irish Governments and of the Northern Ireland Executive-designate, an Executive consisting of representatives of the parties in each community was set up to replace the former Government of Northern Ireland. Agreement was also reached to establish a Council of Ireland to co-ordinate activities in matters of common interest to the Republic and Northern Ireland. The Executive took office in January 1974 but was brought down the following May by a general strike, organised by extreme Unionist political and paramilitary organisations.

Direct rule from Westminister returned and is still in force. A Constitutional Convention which met in 1975-76 failed to produce an agreed report as to the form of government likely to attract widespread support throughout the community. In 1980 a British Government initiative to try to find inter-party agreement in Northern Ireland on a devolved administration was adjourned. In December 1980 the heads of the British and Irish Governments, meeting in Dublin, accepted the need to bring forward policies and proposals to achieve peace, reconciliation and stability. They decided to consider the totality of relationships within these islands and commissioned for that purpose joint studies covering a range of issues.

Chronic unemployment in some urban areas of Northern Ireland has been a constant contributory factor to discontent and rejection of authority. Many of the areas concerned are contiguous to the border and the Irish and British Governments are engaged in a series of joint projects and studies aimed at developing the infrastructures of these areas and promoting the economic well-being of the people north and south.

Government

Under the Northern Ireland Act, 1974, the government of Northern Ireland is exercised through a Secretary of State, appointed by the British Government, who retains responsibility for constitutional matters, security and law and order, and who exercises a special responsibility in overall social and economic planning. A central secretariat carries out on behalf of the Secretary of State the co-ordination of departmental activities where necessary, organises the business of several interdepartmental committees and working groups and provides the main point of liaison with the Northern Ireland Office. There are eight Government Departments: Agriculture, Civil Service, Commerce, Education, Environment, Finance, Health and Social Services and Manpower Services.

There are twenty-six district councils in Northern Ireland responsible for local services such as sanitary, recreational, social, community and cultural facilities, the promotion of tourism and the enforcement of building regulations. The councils are elected by proportional representation on the basis of the single transferable vote.

Courts and Police

The superior courts in Northern Ireland consist of the Supreme Court and the Court of Criminal Appeal. The Supreme Court consists of the High Court, which is the superior court of first instance, and the Court of Appeal, which is the appellate tribunal with power to review the decisions of the High Court. Subject to certain restrictions, judgements of the Appeal Court and the Court of Criminal Appeal can be transferred to the British House of Lords. The inferior courts are the County Courts, which have jurisdiction in most civil and criminal matters, and Magistrates' Courts, which deal with minor civil and criminal cases. Appeal from the Magistrates' Courts lies to the County Courts and from the County Courts to the Supreme Court.

In December 1972 the Commission to consider legal procedures to deal with terrorist activities in Northern Ireland (chairman Lord Diplock) recommended the establishment of non-jury courts to deal with certain offences. These courts, which were set up under the Northern Ireland (Emergency Provisions) Act 1973, are presided over by a single judge and try, on indictment, certain types of offences. The work of these courts was the subject of a review committee under Lord Gardiner, whose report was published in 1975.

The police force, the Royal Ulster Constabulary, consists of a Chief Constable, three Deputy Chief Constables, seven Assistant Chief Constables and 6,850 other ranks. There is also a Royal Ulster Constabulary Reserve which has 3,150 part-time and 1,600 full-time members.

The Defence Forces of Northern Ireland are those of the United Kingdom.

Economy

Industry

Manufacturing industry employs over 140,000 people. The largest group is that of engineering and related industries, which employ almost 50,000. This includes major traditional industries such as ship-building, textile machinery and a growing amount of new, highly diversified production. The construction industry employs 46,000. The textile group of industries employs 33,300 and includes linen, cotton and man-made fibre goods, while the clothing industry employs over 16,000 and includes a large number of shirt and pyjama manufacturers in the Derry area. About 21,000 are involved in the manufacture of food, drink and tobacco products.

Agriculture

About 1.1 million hectares, or 85% of the total land area, are used for agriculture, and a further 60,000 hectares, or 5% are woodland. Most land is held in fee simple, with about 20% being let seasonally. The total number of persons employed in agriculture is about 58,000. In 1977, gross agricultural output (plus production grants) was £494 million.

Services

The largest employment sector is the services sector which employs 340,000 or 58% of the workforce. Apart from the public service which employs 280,000, the most important services are the distributive trades which employ 65,000 and transport and communications which employ 22,000.

Trade

The bulk of Northern Ireland's trade is with Britain. Because exports to and imports from other countries are often through Britain, it is difficult to obtain accurate trade figures.

80. Harland and Wolff's shipyard in Belfast which builds all types of ships, from giant oil tankers to bulk carriers, oil product carriers, vehicle ferries and liquefied gas carriers. Harland and Wolff Ltd also produce marine engines, electrical goods and motor cycle accessories. The giant cranes shown in the picture are each capable of lifting 840 tonnes.

Industrial output by sector to 1981
(1975 = 100)

All Industries	95
Manufacturing Industries	93
Textiles	65
Clothing	100
Engineering & Metals	93
Food, Drink Tobacco	103
Timber, Furniture	79
Mineral Products	69
Other Manufacturing	117
Gas, Electricity Water	117
Construction	103 (1980)

Services

In 1978-79, total revenue (including special payments from the British Exchequer of £568 million) was £1,566 million. Expenditure in that year included £289 million on health and personal social services, £257 million on education, libraries and arts and £90 million on housing. Local Government services are financed from rates, Government grants and loans.

Health and Social Security

The health and social security services in Northern Ireland are similar to those obtaining in Great Britain and are administered by the Northern Ireland Department of Health and Social Services. There are four Health and Social Services Boards, based on the local authority districts, which undertake the area administration of services on behalf of the Department on an integrated basis. There are 82 hospitals with 18,000 beds. There are about 720 doctors on the Boards' lists and the average number of patients per doctor is about 2,200. There are approximately 310 dentists in contract with the Boards.

Housing

In 1979, 7,250 new dwellings were completed in Northern Ireland. These included 3,440 Northern Ireland Housing Executive and 3,570 private enterprise houses. The Housing Executive is the sole public housing authority. Its main functions are the building and management of all publicly-owned housing in Northern Ireland and dealing with unfit housing regardless of ownership. The Department of the Environment has responsibility for the formulation and direction of housing policy and is the planning authority.

Education

There are a total of 1,080 primary schools with a combined total enrolment of 204,200 pupils and 8,480 teachers are employed in these. At the second level, there are grammar schools with an academic orientation and intermediate schools with a curriculum combining general and practical subjects. The 21 State and 57 voluntary grammar schools have 57,600 pupils, while the 92 State and 91 voluntary secondary intermediate schools have 106,200 pupils. There are 10,350 full-time teachers employed in these second level schools. There are two technical colleges providing commercial and technical education for full-time and part-time students. The Ulster Polytechnic Belfast, which provides higher non-university education, has 4,000 full-time students and 3,000 part-time students.

Northern Ireland has two universities, the Queen's University of Belfast (1845) with 5,800 students and the New University of Ulster at Coleraine (1970) with 1,750 students.

Newspapers and Periodicals

There are two morning daily newspapers in Northern Ireland: *The News Letter* (circulation 61,000) and *The Irish News* (47,500), and one evening daily, *The Belfast Telegraph* (152,000). All three are published in Belfast. *The News Letter* is the oldest extant newspaper in Ireland, having been founded in 1737. *The News Letter* also publishes the only Northern Irish Sunday newspaper, *The Sunday News* (89,000). In addition, forty-one local newspapers are published throughout Northern Ireland, one twice-weekly, the others weekly. A number of periodicals is published, covering business, professional and leisure interests.

Radio and Television

Northern Ireland has seven radio stations, six operated by the British Broadcasting Corporation (BBC) (Radios 1, 2, 3 and 4, Radio Ulster and Radio Foyle) and Downtown Radio, Belfast, a commercial radio station operated by the Independent Broadcasting Authority. Both of these authorities also provide local television services, BBC 1 and BBC 2 and Ulster Television (UTV).

Culture

Language

The Irish language was until late in the first half of the 19th century the language of the majority of the population. Despite periodic efforts to encourage its use, it has lost ground steadily to English and is now spoken as an everyday language in limited areas, mainly along the western seaboard, known collectively as the *Gaeltacht*. The total number of native speakers living in *Gaeltacht* areas is currently estimated at about 55,000.

Irish is a Celtic language closely related to Scottish Gaelic and Manx and more distantly to Welsh, Breton and Cornish. It presents a number of unique features among Indo-European languages including a rich sound system in which consonantal sounds have palatal and velar varieties. Nouns, verbs and adjectives are inflected and, in common with other Celtic languages, undergo initial mutations.

The earliest records of Irish are found in funerary stones inscribed with a variant of the Latin alphabet known as *Ogham* and datable to about the fourth century AD. Apart from *Ogham* inscriptions, the earliest texts are legal tracts, glosses on Latin texts and fragments of poetry. Though preserved in later manuscripts, the language of some of these texts is datable to the sixth century and shows considerable changes from the archaic language of the *Ogham* stones. It was, however, a remarkably standardised language. Under the unsettled conditions of the Viking times, the transition to Middle Irish took place. A new standardised language again appears in Early Modern Irish (1250-1650) but with the collapse of the Gaelic order after Cromwell, literature appears in the modern vernacular in its three main dialects (Ulster, Connacht and Munster).

Irish vocabulary owes much to various external influences through the centuries. There are earlier borrowings from the unknown language of the pre-Celtic peoples, the Latin and Welsh of the early Christian missionaries, the Norse of the Vikings, the French of the Normans and finally, the greatest

Language

influence of all, English, the language of the settlers and, ultimately, of the majority of the Irish people.

The precarious position of Irish in the last century inspired Douglas Hyde to found the Gaelic League (1893) with the object of arresting the decline. The League was unsuccessful in this but did succeed in arousing an abiding concern for the language in many outside the *Gaeltacht*. Irish is now an official language of the State and is taught in all schools.

Roinn na Gaeltachta (The Department of the *Gaeltacht*), established in 1956, has the function of promoting the welfare of the *Gaeltacht* and encouraging wider use of Irish. Under its auspices there are two statutory bodies, *Bord na Gaeilge* (Board for Irish), the role of which is to promote the Irish language and, in particular, its use as a living language and *Údarás na Gaeltachta* (Gaeltacht Authority), which encourages the use of the Irish language as the principal medium of communication in the *Gaeltacht* and promotes the general development of the *Gaeltacht.*

English has been spoken in Ireland probably since the 12th century when English servants and artisans accompanied the French-speaking Normans to Ireland. French ceased to be spoken by the Normans in the 14th century, and was replaced for official legal purposes by English in the later Middle Ages. The use of English was largely confined to the towns until the collapse of the Gaelic order in the 17th century, after which by its monopoly in law and commerce it gradually spread throughout the countryside. Its diffusion was particularly rapid after the Great Famine of the mid-19th century.

English as spoken in Ireland retains many characteristics of an earlier period and contains a Gaelic substratum in pronunciation, intonation, vocabulary and phrasing. The English of the Northern part of the country shows in addition some strong Scottish influences. Traces of a particularly distinctive dialect of English remain in parts of Co. Wexford.

THE
SHANACHIE

Folklore

The traditional Irish outlook on life is best illustrated by a study of folk belief and custom reflecting the mind of the people throughout the ages. Many facets of folk belief which have vanished elsewhere are still to be found in Ireland.

Ireland has one of the richest bodies of traditional lore in Europe and one of the largest collections of folklore recorded in the early decades of this century on manuscript, disc and later on tape.

Irish folklore includes tales, legends, stave-anecdotes, poetry, proverbs, prayers and riddles. Many of these are still to be found in living tradition. Other aspects of traditional Irish life associated with pastimes (music, song, dance and games) have also lived on until now despite outside influence.

The Irish Folklore Commission (1935-71), now incorporated in the Department of Irish Folklore at University College, Dublin, has undertaken considerable work in the collection, presentation, classification, study and exposition of all aspects of the Irish folk tradition.

83. A detail of The Gathering of the Armies, one of the brush drawings by the distinguished Irish artist, Louis le Brocquy, which illustrated the English translation of Táin Bó Cuailnge by the poet, Thomas Kinsella (Dublin, The Dolmen Press, 1969).

Literature in Irish

Literature in Irish, to which we can ascribe a date, first appears in the sixth century in poems of praise, satire and laments written by professional poets, heirs to the pre-Christian druids. These were preserved in manuscripts copied by the early Irish monks who themselves produced lyric poetry of a high quality. Their verse displays an acute feeling for language and an impressionistic treatment of their themes reminiscent of certain eastern literatures. The monks also preserved compilations of the traditional orally transmitted literature which contain much material from the pre-Christian period. These include the heroic and mythological sagas such as *Táin Bó Cuailnge,* a work of great strength (and indeed a source of inspiration to modern writers such as Pearse) which is also of particular value for the light it throws on early Irish society. Much of our knowledge of Irish mythology derives from the saga *Cath Maige Tured* Irish literature of this period was not without influence on later European literature. The theme of tragic love, best illustrated in the legend of Tristan and Isolde, derives from Irish sources. A genre of adventure stories provided the source for the Arthurian legends, while accounts of voyages such as *Immram Curaigh Maíle Dúin* and the Latin *Navigatio Brendani* also captured the imagination of medieval Europe.

Literary creativity received a setback with the Norse incursions and the early Norman invasion. The chief works of the Middle Irish period (900-1250) are the beautiful and original *Buile Shuibhne* and *Aisling Meic Conglinne,* a trenchant and humorous satire on life in the 12th century.

The Early Modern period (1250-1650) is characterised by the emergence of the modern language, albeit in a highly standardised literary version. We have a large body of verse known as bardic poetry from this period written by bards trained for up to twelve years in bardic schools in the use of the most intricate metres according to strict rules. Most of this poetry is encomiastic

95

84

85

84 and 85. Two woodcuts illustrating the Navigatio Brendani (Voyage of St Brendan) from Sankt Brandans Seefahrt, printed in Augsburg, in 1476. The reproductions here are from a translation by Professor John J O'Meara (Dublin, The Dolmen Press, 1976).

Literature in Irish

commemoration of his patron by the poet but there is much religious and personal poetry of quality.

In this period, prose and poetry centering on the legends of Fionn Mac Cumhaill, his son Oisín, and their warrier band, the Fianna, emerge from folklore into literature in *Agallamh na Seanórach*. The legends survive to the present day in folklore both in Ireland and in Gaelic Scotland where McPherson found the sources of his Ossianic forgeries which so impressed the early Romantic movement in Europe. The Irish revolutionaries of the second half of the 19th century called themselves Fenians after the Fianna.

The Early Modern period ended with Geoffrey Keating's great prose history *Foras Feasa ar Eirinn* written just before the Gaelic order received its death-blow from Cromwell. After the Early Modern period, the language of the people comes into its own. Much of the material of the late 17th century relates to the political events of the time. The Cromwellian settlers and the new order are mercilessly satirised in the anonymous prose work *Pairlimint Chloinne Thomáis* and in the poetry of Dáibhidh Ó Bruadair (1625-98). The greatest of the new poets, Aogán Ó Rathaile (1670-1726), lamented the passing of the old order in powerful verse. He was the last of the aristocratic poets and was followed by men of the people. At the time of the Penal Laws, the poet saw visions of better times to come, a genre best exemplified by Eoghan Ruadh Ó Súilleabháin (1748-84), who poured forth a torrent of imaginative and musical verse. Daniel O'Connell's aunt, Éibhlín Dubh Ní Chonaill (1748-1800), lamented her husband, a victim of the Penal Laws, in the magnificent poem, *Caoine Airt Uí Laoire*. The 18th century closed with the long Rabelaisian poem of great originality, *Cúirt an Mheán Oíche* by Brian Merriman (1747-1805), a work which has attracted many translators. The traditional literature had its last great exponent before the trauma of the Great Famine in 'Raftery', a blind

Literature in Irish

fiddler, Antoine Ó Reachtabhra (1784-1835).

The revival of the national consciousness towards the end of the 19th century inspired a number of writers who gradually made the transition from traditional to contemporary European models. Some such as Peadar Ó Laoire (1839-1929) took their inspiration from folklore and the sagas of Old Irish. Pádraic Pearse (1879-1916) applied European standards to his poetry, prose and drama while deeply conscious of the heritage of the past. The novelist, Pádraic Ó Conaire (1882-1928), wrote short stories of quality on the model of Chekhov.

Among contemporary writers, poetry flourishes in the evocative lyrics of Máirtín Ó Direáin (1910-   ), the cerebral and imaginative work of Seán Ó Ríordáin (1917-77), and the sensitive love poetry of Máire Mhac an tSaoi (1922-   ). Prose writers tend to favour the short story but the novel is well represented, most powerfully in *Cré na Cille,* a work of great range and complexity by Máirtín Ó Cadhain (1907-70). Drama and criticism are to be found in the works of Seán Ó Tuama (1926-   ).

The continuity of literature in the Irish language over fifteen centuries is a source of pride to Irish writers today. The range and vitality of the literature at the present moment, when one considers the catastrophic decline of the spoken language, is truly remarkable.

86. Pádraic Ó Conaire

87. Máirtín Ó Direáin

88. Seán Ó Ríordáin

89. Máire Mhac an tSaoi

90. Máirtín Ó Cadhain

91. Seán Ó Tuama

86
87

88
89

90
91

99

92. The Emperor of
Lilliput Reviews his
Troops, *an
illustration by Arthur
Rackham for*
Gulliver's Travels *by
Jonathan Swift.*

Literature in English

The English language came to Ireland with the
followers of the earliest Norman settlers. The
English-speaking community remained small and
confined to a restricted area around Dublin and other
cities until the collapse of the Gaelic order at the
beginning of the 17th century.

Some early lyrics which were written in Ireland have
survived from the beginning of the 13th century
together with some satirical poems such as *The
Land of Cokaygne.* These poems, while in English,
have resemblances to satirical works in Irish such as
Aisling Meic Conglinne.

The first great Anglo-Irish writer was Jonathan Swift
(1667-1745) who produced a considerable body of
political and social satire. These included *A Tale of a
Tub, The Battle of the Books* and his masterpiece
Gulliver's Travels. His *Drapier's Letters* had an
important influence on Irish political developments at
the time.

Edmund Burke (1729-97), though first and foremost
a great parliamentarian, was also an important
political philosopher. Through his writings and
speeches, especially *Reflections on the Revolution in
France,* he exerted considerable influence both on
19th century romantic historians and on the
development of political conservatism. For the
aesthetic theory of the 19th century his *Philosophical
Enquiry into the Origin of our Ideas of the Sublime
and Beautiful* was important.

Towards the end of the 18th century, Irish writing in
English (with the exception of drama) began to deal
with more specifically local themes and concerns.
Castle Rackrent by Maria Edgeworth (1767-1849),
published in 1800, was the first novel that dealt
specifically with Irish life. Her influence as the
originator of the regional novel on authors such as
Scott and Turgenev was considerable. Other Irish
novelists in this tradition were William Carleton
(1794-1869) and Charles James Lever (1806-72).

Literature in English

The poetry of Thomas Moore (1779-1852) opened up a period in Anglo-Irish literature which was romantic and nationalist in inspiration. The rise of Irish nationalism in the 19th century had the effect of encouraging a rediscovery of Gaelic culture and literature aided by the work of scholars such as Eugene O'Curry and John O'Donovan. Later poets such as James Clarence Mangan (1803-49), Thomas Davis (1814-45) and Samuel Ferguson (1810-86) wrote stirring verse on Irish legendary themes and made verse translations of Irish poetry. These works, with the added impetus of Standish O'Grady's popularisations of early Irish sagas, had a considerable influence on the young William Butler Yeats (1865-1939), around whom a great literary revival gathered and blossomed. The influence of these earlier writers, and his associations with nationalist figures such as the Fenian, John O'Leary, brought about a change in the direction of Yeats' poetry from pre-Raphaelitism to include more specifically Irish themes. Other leading writers of the Literary Revival included the poets and novelists George Moore (1852-1933), George Russell ('AE') (1867-1935), Pádraic Colum (1881-1973) and James Stephens (1882-1950).

The work of James Joyce (1882-1941) has been a major influence on world literature. His four main works, *Dubliners, A Portrait of the Artist as a Young Man, Ulysses* and *Finnegans Wake* are all set in his native Dublin. The last two works are distinguished by their complex structure, concentrated language, wealth of motif and association and original use of modern narrative techniques. The comic genius of Flann O'Brien (1912-66) found its expression in a number of novels (of which the best known is *At Swim Two Birds*) and other writings. He was considerably influenced by the writings of Joyce.

The most significant poets of the generation after Yeats include Austin Clarke (1890-1974), Patrick Kavanagh (1906-67) and Louis MacNeice (1907-63). Among contemporary poets, a greater

Literature in English

range of influences and wider concerns may be discerned while their work attempts to come to terms with the present state of the country and its historical roots. This is particularly true of the works of Richard Murphy (1927-   ), Thomas Kinsella (1928-   ), John Montague (1929-   ), Brendan Kennelly (1936-   ), Seamus Heaney (1939-   ), Derek Mahon (1941-   ) and Hugh Maxton (1947-   ).

Perhaps the most remarkable achievement of the generation of writers who followed Yeats lay in the sphere of the short story. Here Liam O'Flaherty (1896-   ), Seán Ó Faoláin (1900-   ) and Frank O'Connor (1903-66) created short stories of the highest level. This tradition is being maintained at present by writers such as Bryan McMahon (1909-   ), Mary Lavin (1912-   ), Benedict Kiely (1919-   ), James Plunkett (1920-   ) and many others. In the period since the Second World War, and particularly in the last ten years, Irish fiction has moved towards a greater flexibility of technique and subject matter. The broadening of national horizons has been reflected in the cosmopolitan settings, the greater scope and more wide-ranging affinities of contemporary fiction. Francis Stuart (1902-   ), Brian Moore (1921-   ), Aidan Higgins (1927-   ), John McGahern (1935-   ) and John Banville (1945-   ) are among the most notable contemporary writers.

Drama
There is a strong tradition of drama among Anglo-Irish writers dating back to the early 17th century. Many later dramatists had a powerful influence on the development of the English theatre for which they wrote.

In addition to his plays, *The Good-Natur'd Man* and *She Stoops to Conquer,* Oliver Goldsmith (1728-74) is also known for his novel, *The Vicar of Wakefield,* and a poem, *The Deserted Village.* Before turning to a political career at Westminster, Richard Brinsley

Literature in English

Sheridan (1751-1816) held the London stage with his three great comedies, *The Rivals, The Critic* and his masterpiece, *The School for Scandal.* The dominant Irish dramatist in the 19th century was Oscar Wilde (1856-1900) who captivated London audiences of the 1890s with his brilliant comedies, *Lady Windermere's Fan, A Woman of No Importance, An Ideal Husband* and *The Importance of Being Earnest.*

The plays of George Bernard Shaw (1856-1950) such as *Arms and the Man, The Doctor's Dilemma, Man and Superman, Androcles and the Lion* and *St Joan,* have earned him a place among the great playwrights in the English language. Yeats' plays, experimental and short for the most part, are less well-known than his poetry, but his influence on the theatre in Ireland has been considerable. With Lady Gregory (1859-1932) and Edward Martyn (1859-1923) he founded the Abbey Theatre Company in 1904, which launched two major dramatists, John Millington Synge (1871-1909) and Seán O'Casey (1880-1964). Synge's genius lay in bringing rural speech, customs and thought to effective dramatic dialogue in plays such as *Riders to the Sea* and *The Playboy of the Western World.* O'Casey brought the working class to the stage for the first time, most remarkably in his plays, *The Shadow of a Gunman, Juno and the Paycock* and *The Plough and the Stars.* Other dramatists whose plays were performed at the Abbey were TC Murray (1873-1959), Lennox Robinson (1886-1958), George Shiels (1881-1949) and Pádraic Colum (1881-1972). The autobiography, *Borstal Boy,* and two plays, *The Quare Fellow* and *The Hostage,* are regarded as the most enduring work of Brendan Behan (1923-1964) whose work is distinguished by his humane feeling for individual victims and by an exuberant delight in language, song and comedy of incident.

Samuel Beckett (1906-   ) is the Irish dramatist best known internationally. He has been awarded the

100
101
102
103
104
105

Literature in English

Nobel Prize for Literature, as were Yeats and Shaw previously. He first earned his international reputation with the play, *Waiting for Godot,* and the trilogy of novels, *Molloy, Malone Dies* and *The Unnamable. All that Fall, Endgame, Krapp's Last Tape* and *Happy Days* are among the best known of his later plays. A number of younger playwrights, including Hugh Leonard (1928-   ), John B Keane (1928-   ), Brian Friel (1929-   ), Eugene McCabe (1930-   ) and Tom Murphy (1936-   ) are producing work of a high quality, and several of their plays have been successful abroad as well as in Ireland.

The National Theatre Society based at the Abbey Theatre stages primarily Irish drama. The Gate Theatre Company founded by Mícheál MacLiammóir and Hilton Edwards in 1928 produces a variety of Irish and foreign plays. Denis Johnston (1901-   ), best known for his play, *The Old Lady Says 'No',* is one of the more important dramatists whose work was first produced at the Gate. The Project Arts Company emphasises experimental drama. The extraordinarily high standard of the extensive amateur drama movement and the proliferation of fringe and pub theatres are important factors in the vitality of contemporary Irish theatre. Drama in Ireland is assisted by the State.

Repertory companies, especially that of Anew McMaster, formed an important part of Irish cultural life in the first half of the century. In 1974, the State revived this tradition with the establishment of the Irish Theatre Company, bringing professional theatre to audiences outside the larger centres.

A National Folk Theatre, *Siamsa Tíre*, was established at Tralee in 1972.

The Dublin Theatre Festival, held annually in October, is the highlight of Irish theatrical life.

Birmingham
REP

Birmingham Repertory Theatre
Broad Street
Birmingham B1 2EP
Box Office 021-236 4455

BRUM STUDIO

27 March –
27 April

WAITING FOR
GODOT

SAMUEL BECKETT

Art

The earliest Irish art is found in abstract geometric
carvings in the megalithic tombs of the Boyne Valley,
which date from 2500-2000 BC.

The La Tène art of the Celts, found in Ireland
towards the end of the Bronze Age, characterised
much of Irish art in early historical times. The Celts
excelled in refinement of detail and delicacy of line,
preferring stylisation to direct representation in their
treatment of animate subjects.

By the seventh century AD, Irish art had undergone
many developments. Improvements in filigree and
enamel technique in metalwork, with greater carving
relief and narrative pictorial treatment in sculpture,
coincided with new applications in ecclesiastical art:
high crosses, reliquaries, chalices and bookshrines. It
was, however, in the development of a distinctive
and highly elaborate style of illuminated manuscripts
that the vernacular Celtic style reached its fullest
development between the seventh and the ninth
centuries.

The Book of Durrow (circa 650) with its subdued
tones and subtle use of space and ornament
represents the apex of one tradition, while the
somewhat later Book of Kells, with its altogether
more lavish ornamentation is the chief treasure of
Celtic art in Ireland.

The large stone High Crosses, over 150 of which
still survive, were a distinctive Irish creation. Some of
the best examples may date from the ninth century.
Their carved panels, depicting biblical scenes, were a
form of visual religious instruction. The finest is the
Cross of Muiredach at Monasterboice, Co. Louth.

Reciprocal influences between Irish and Viking art
are in evidence from the mid-ninth century. In the
11th and 12th centuries considerable technical and
decorative elements from both Scandinavian and
Continental Romanesque art were absorbed into the
traditional art.

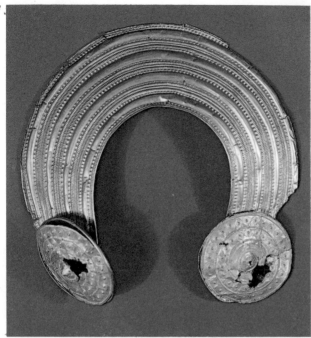

108. The Borrisnoe (Co. Tipperary) gold collar from the National Museum of Ireland, which contains the largest collection of prehistoric gold objects found in western and northern Europe.

109. A golden boat found at Broighter, Co. Derry. It may date from the first century AD.

110. The Tara Brooch, a fine ring-brooch of silver with embellishments of gold, amber and multicoloured glass. It dates from the eighth century AD.

111. The Ardagh Chalice, also from the eighth century, is made of silver with inlaid panels of gold, silver chainmesh and copper, with studs of amber and glass of different colours. The names of the Apostles, in Latin, are etched lightly into the surface of the bowl.

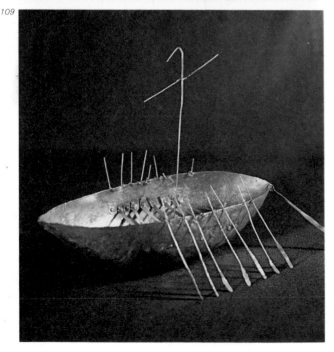

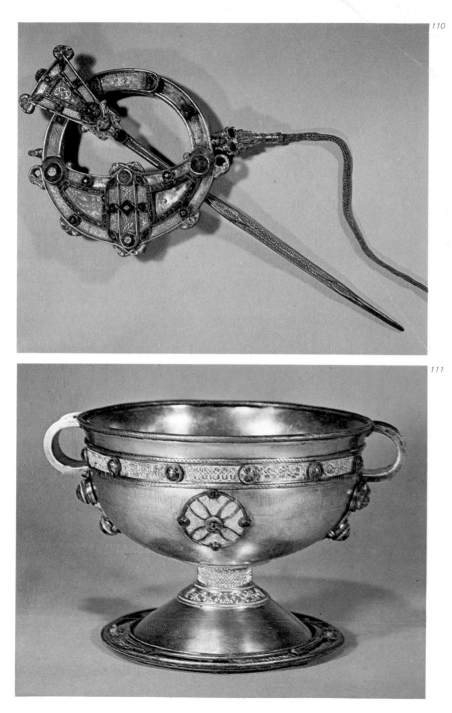

113

112. Muiredach's Cross at Monasterboice, Co. Louth, the finest of the stone High Crosses which were erected in Ireland from the 7th to the 12th centuries. Many are carved with panels showing scenes from the Scriptures. Those in Muiredach's Cross include the Arrest of Christ, Doubting Thomas and the Crucifixion.

113. The doorway of Clonfert Cathedral, the greatest achievement of Irish Romanesque decoration.

114. A stone carving of an owl from the interior of Holy Cross Abbey, one of the finest examples of the late Gothic style to survive in Ireland.

115. A panel from the High Cross at Moone, Co. Kildare.

116. The stone rib vaulting in the roof of the shrine at Holy Cross Abbey.

117. The flamboyant tomb at Kilconnel Friary, an excellent example of Gothic funerary sculpture.

Art

Parallel with the period of Irish Gothic architecture, a
distinctive Gothic sculpture was developed which
found its finest expression in funerary monuments of
the 15th century, especially those associated with
Rory O'Tunney in south Leinster and Munster.
Polychrome wood sculpture also thrived at this time,
particularly in Connacht.

Growing contacts between Ireland and Continental
Europe during the 16th and 17th centuries brought
about the gradual introduction of classicism into Irish
art, and from about the mid-17th century there was
a brilliant flowering of the decorative arts,
plasterwork, furniture, silver and glass in conjunction
with the large-scale building activity of the time.

By the middle of the 17th century, easel painting
was firmly established and had displaced tapestries
and wall painting as the principal decorative art. In
1670, a painters' guild was incorporated in Dublin.
Garrett Morphey (d. 1716) and James Latham
(1696-1747) who had studied at Antwerp
dominated Irish painting in the early 18th century.
The more important painters of the latter part of the
century include Robert Hunter (fl. 1748-1803) and
James Barry (1741-1806), a friend of Edmund
Burke.

Romanticism reached its height in the early and mid-
19th century with the genre painter, William
Mulready (1786-1863), Daniel Maclise (1803-70),
who specialised in historical subjects, and the
landscape painter, Francis Danby (1793-1861).

The impact of impressionism in Irish art is already
apparent in the work of Nathaniel Hone
(1813-1917), John Butler Yeats (1839-1922),
Sarah Purser (1884-1943) and Roderick O'Conor
(1860-1940), but the foremost Irish representative
of the movement was Jack B Yeats (1871-1957),
who together with Walter Osborne (1859-1903)
and William Orpen (1878-1931), dominated artistic
life in Ireland in the early part of this century. The

The harp crowned.
This certified that the
metal was of
standard fineness.

The date letter
indicting the year
during which the
piece was made.

The marker's mark:
usually the maker's
initials stamped on
the piece before
being sent for assay.

The figure of
Hibernia, a female
figure symbolising
Ireland. Although
originally a duty
mark, it can now be
regarded as the
special mark of the

Dublin Goldsmiths'
Company. Another
duty mark, the
monarch's head,
was introduced in
1807, but was
discontinued from
1890 when the duty
was abolished.

118. Kettle, Stand
and Lamp, silver, by
William Townsend,
Dublin, about 1735.
These kettles held
about six pints. They
were usually
provided with a
stand which was
fitted with a spirit
burner to keep water
hot at table. It was
necessary at the time
to have hot water
close at hand as
teapots then were
small and had to be
refilled perhaps
several times.

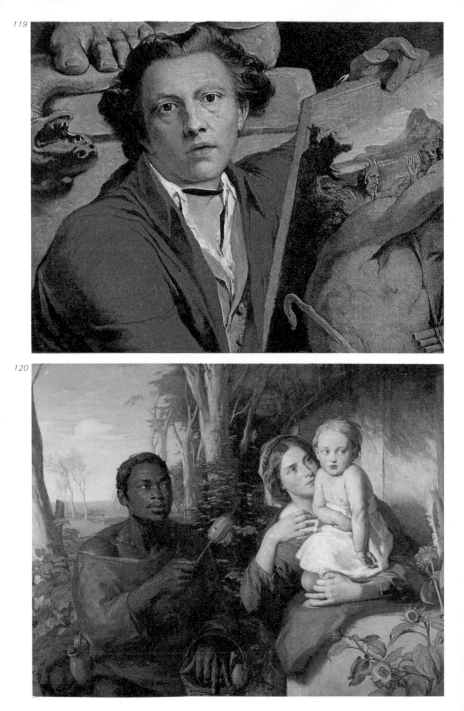

119. *A detail of*
Self-Portrait, *1803,*
by James Barry.

120. The Toy-Seller
by William Mulready.

121. Portrait of a
Lady *by James*
Latham.

122. *A detail of* The
Washerwoman *by*
William Orpen.

121

122

Art

123. A detail of The Liffey Swim *by Jack B Yeats.*

124. Scene in the Phoenix Park *by Walter Osborne.*

movements of the twenties and thirties such as surrealism, cubism and abstractionism, attracted a new generation of artists, including Mainie Jellett, Evie Hone, Norah McGuinness and Louis le Brocquy.

Although there are common elements in the work of most contemporary Irish artists, the range and variety of their output reflects the situation in present-day art throughout the world. There are, of course, distinctive Irish influences also, particularly from the past, for instance, in Louis le Brocquy's narrative black brush drawings for Thomas Kinsella's translation of the *Táin*, in Anne Madden's series *Megaliths* and *Standing Stones* and in the soft colours of Patrick Scott's tempera paintings. Contemporary political themes appear in the works of young artists such as Robert Ballagh and Micheal Farrell.

The 19th century was a very active period in Irish sculpture, best represented in the work of John Hogan (1800-58) and John Henry Foley (1819-74). In this century, sculpture continues as a strong element in artistic expression, including the historic treatment found in the works of Seamus Murphy, Edward Delaney and Oisín Kelly, and the abstractionism of Hilary Heron, Deborah Brown and John Burke.

The revival of church building after Catholic Emancipation (1829) contributed to the growth of an Irish school of stained glass, beginning in the 1850s. A number of studios today produce glass which is sought world-wide. Those principally responsible for this development were Michael Healy (1873-1941), Harry Clarke (1889-1931) and Evie Hone (1894-1955).

Artists in Ireland receive considerable assistance from the State. *An Chomairle Ealaíon* (The Arts Council) advises the Government on matters relating to the arts. The Council provides artists with a guaranteed income and administers a scheme for honouring

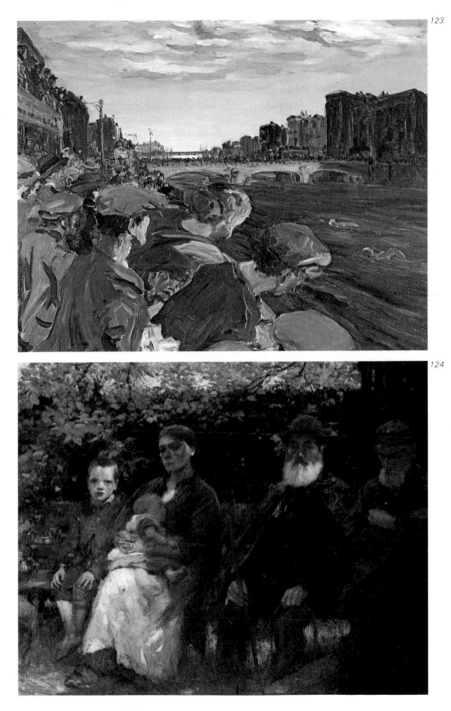

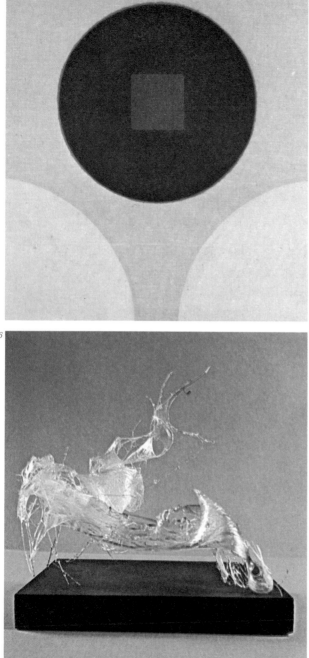

125

126

125. Painting Object 5, 1972, *(tempera on canvas) by Patrick Scott.*

126. Glass Fibre Form, 1974, *(glass fibre sculpture in perspex box) by Deborah Brown.*

127. Pressé Series Real *(acrylic and cut-out canvas on timber) by Micheal Farrell.*

128. Megalith Series No. 14, 1971, *(diptych, polymer acrylic on cotton duck) by Anne Madden.*

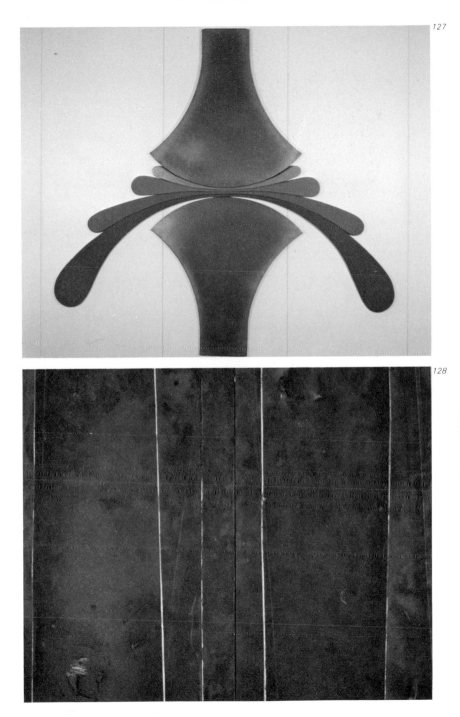

Art

established artists in the fields of literature, music and the visual arts through the *Aosdána* organisation. Other artists are encouraged by bursaries. The Cultural Relations Committee of the Department of Foreign Affairs assists in the promotion of artists and their work outside the country.

Annual public exhibitions were inaugurated by the Society of Artists in Ireland in 1764, and the Royal Hibernian Academy held its first annual exhibition in 1826. In 1864, the National Gallery was opened in Dublin and in 1885 a municipal gallery was opened in Cork. A contemporary art gallery was opened in Dublin in 1908.

The National College of Art and Design has its origins in the Academy for Drawing and Painting established by the Dublin Society in 1746. The College, which is now under the Department of Education, provides a diploma course in Fine Arts and Design. There are departments of the History of Art at UCD and TCD. Outside Dublin City, the Vocational Education Committees operate schools of art at Cork, Dún Laoghaire, Limerick and Waterford.

129. A detail of St Julian *by Harry Clarke. One of the rare miniature stained glass panels made by him, it is only 5" x 8½" and consists of two unleaded pieces of flashed ruby and blue glass plated together, acided, etched and painted. As well as perfecting this unique technique, Harry Clarke was an extraordinarily imaginative decorative artist and book illustrator.*

130. The entrance to Newgrange, one of the finest passage graves in western Europe. On the left can be seen a triple spiral geometric decoration, unique in Newgrange.

131. The Grianán *of* Aileach, *probably built in the early Christian era in Ireland. Its hill-top position gives it an excellent view of Lough Foyle and Lough Swilly. The wall is 13 feet thick and contains small chambers. The fort served as the royal seat of the O'Neill sept of Aileach possibly from the 5th to the 12th conturios.*

Architecture

The earliest man-made structures still visible in the Irish countryside date from the Stone Age. The most spectacular of these, exhibiting great engineering ingenuity, are megalithic tombs. The passage grave at Newgrange, dating from about 2500 BC, is one of the best-known of these great prehistoric monuments.

Large hill forts and ring forts were built early in the Iron Age (about 500 BC), the most imposing of which were the splendid stone-built ones such as the *Grianán* of Aileach in Co. Donegal and Staigue Fort in Co. Kerry.

A new smaller-scale building form based on prehistoric stone building practice emerged in the early Christian period from about the fifth century AD. A corbelled stone method of walling and roofing was used in the building of monastic settlements, often in remote areas such as the spectacular site on the island of Skellig Michael off the Kerry coast. The other notable monuments of the early Christian period were the elegant, tall, stone round towers. These were built as landmarks and bell-towers, but many have the entrance door placed well above ground level to act as strong places of refuge in case of attack.

In the 12th century, Romanesque architecture flowered with many churches being built throughout the country in a characteristic Irish style using decorative motifs carved in stone. The designs were often fantastic and bizarre. Human heads, animals and deep-cut zig-zag mouldings were common. The most beautiful of these churches is almost certainly the exquisite Cormac's Chapel which nestles beside the larger medieval church on the Rock of Cashel.

The Norman settlers of the late 12th century began a spate of castle building which was to last until the 15th century. The great castle of Trim, Co. Meath, with its tall central keep surrounded by a high defensive wall, was one of many built during this

132

133

132. St Kevin's Church, Glendalough, a nave-and-chancel church with a stone roof and a small round tower which acted as a belfry. The detached round tower to the right of the church is about 100 feet in height, with a door about 10 feet from the ground.

133. Cormac's Chapel, Cashel, built in 1127-34. Its roof is also of stone. The church, which shows the influence of both German and English Romanesque architecture, has a nave and chancel with blind arcades on the walls, a barrel-vault and a fine chancel arch. The stonework, particularly in the interior, is profusely decorated.

134. The former monk's choir and chancel at Holy Cross Abbey, showing the original vaulting, after recent restoration. Founded in the 12th century, much of the Abbey was rebuilt in the 15th century in a distinctively late Gothic style.

Architecture

period. The transitional style of architecture accompanied the introduction of many religious orders to Ireland in the early 13th century. The churches and monasteries built in this style feature pointed arches and arrangements of buildings around a quadrangle. The monasteries at Boyle, Co. Roscommon, and Jerpoint, Co. Kilkenny, are typical of this period.

There was a continuation of defensive building in the 16th century with many tower houses and fortified mansions developing the tradition of the more basic stone castle. However, unfortified town houses were also built. An excellent example, now preserved, is Rothe House in Kilkenny.

The destruction of the Cromwellian Wars virtually ended building in the mid-17th century. However, in the second half of that century, great star-shaped forts in the continental style were built around the coasts and along the Shannon River. The beautiful Royal Hospital at Kilmainham by Sir William Robinson also dates from this period.

Classical architecture came to Ireland in the 18th century with the expansion of the cities and the building of elegant Palladian country houses. Castletown House at Celbridge, Co. Kildare, is one of the finest of these, but many smaller houses in simple style and with fine craftsmanship were built throughout the country. Many public buildings were erected at this time in the cities and towns. The medieval Dublin Castle was largely remodelled in the 1750s, although two of the early towers were incorporated in the new arrangement and are still clearly visible today. The main front of Trinity College was erected in 1759 to complement the imposing Parliament House of 1729, now the Bank of Ireland in College Green, Dublin. Other great Dublin public buildings of the later 18th century included the Four Courts and the Custom House by James Gandon. Francis Johnston's many buildings in Dublin and throughout the country were notable in this period.

135. Bunratty Castle, Co. Clare. Built on the site of previous fortifications, this structure was constructed in the 15th century. Restored in the present century, the castle now contains one of the best collections of 14th- to 17th-century furniture and furnishings in Ireland. Re-enacted medieval banquets take place there now and a Folk Park has been laid out beside it.

136. The Royal Hospital, Kilmainham, Dublin, the most notable building of its time in Ireland. Designed by Sir William Robinson, with arcaded cloisters round a courtyard, it is evidence of Dublin's great expansion in the later 17th century.

137

138

137. The gardens of Powerscourt, one of the country houses designed by Richard Castle, the most influential architect of the first half of the 18th century in Ireland.

138. Two examples of the beautiful doorways from the classical period which are such a distinctive feature of Dublin's architectural heritage.

139. The exterior of Castletown House, the largest and best examples of Irish Palladianism. Designed by Alessandro Galilei for William Conolly, Speaker of the Irish Parliament, it was begun about 1772. The wings, with their curved Ionic colonnades, were designed by Sir Edward Lovett Pearce.

140. An interior of Castletown House. Much of the interior was also designed by Pearce.

Architecture

141. Tynan's Bridge House Bar, Kilkenny, an example of the elaborate shop front which is a feature of Irish towns.

Urban design and town planning flourished with the work of the Dublin Wide Streets Commissioners and the layout of superb Georgian squares and terraces, particularly in Dublin. Many urban spaces in other Irish towns and villages owe their quality to the design and craft of the 18th century. Interior design also flourished, particularly decorative plasterwork and marble and wood carving. An Irish characteristic of the 18th century was the ingenious use of wild and beautiful scenery, visible today in the heritage of superb gardens and estates.

There was a great upsurge in Catholic church building in Ireland in the 19th century and Pugin, the Gothic Revival architect, was influential in this movement. JJ McCarthy promoted many of the ideas of Pugin in a long list of churches in towns all over the country. The Church of Ireland architect, John Semple, working in a very striking and individual style of Plain Gothic, built many fine churches in the Dublin area.

For many centuries the characteristic dwelling in country areas was the single-storey 'long house' built of local materials. Clay or stone was used for the walls and this was plastered or lime-washed for weatherproofing. The roof was covered with various types of thatch depending on local availability, grass sods, reeds or straw, often tied down to resist the strong winds.

In the small towns and villages, well-proportioned terraces of neat, stone-built houses still provide good homes and their pitched roofs and window patterns give a special character to the towns.

In the 20th century, the main cities and towns have expanded with commercial and community buildings. Hospitals, schools and factories have been added to the older stock of building and new housing estates have been provided for the urban areas. Irish architects are actively involved in solving the many problems of providing a good environment

142

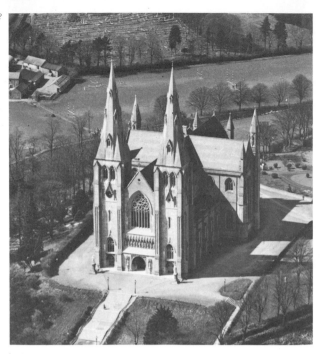

143

142. St Patrick's Cathedral, Armagh, largely designed by JJ McCarthy.

143. The National Museum of Ireland, photographed about 1895. Designed by Sir Thomas Manly Deane, it was begun in 1884 as was the matching building which houses the National Library of Ireland.

144. A cottage with thatched roof near Ballinakill, Co. Galway, the characteristic type of rural dwelling in Ireland up to the present century.

145. A detail of the model of the Roundstone Project by the firm of Stephenson and Associates. Roundstone, a village of 200 people in a beautiful and remote area on Ireland's west coast was chosen by the Industrial Development Authority as a pilot scheme in a programme aimed at relating small-scale manufacturing craftsmanship and housing to each other, to the village and the landscape in general.

Architecture

for present-day society in Ireland. Many firms have also carried out commissions overseas, particularly in the Middle East and Africa.

There are two Schools of Architecture in Dublin, at University College and at the College of Technology, Bolton Street. The Royal Institute of the Architects of Ireland (1893) regulates the practice of architecture.

146. A section of the Irish Life Centre, Dublin, designed by the firm of Robinson, Keefe and Devane. This modern comprehensive urban development includes offices, shops and residential units with facilities for recreation and amenity.

Music

The importance of music in Irish cultural life is attested by the written accounts of Irish music from the pre-modern period. The harp was the dominant and characteristic instrument in historical times, and was adopted as the arms of Ireland in the 17th century. One of the few early composers whose work has survived was the poet, harpist and composer, Turlough O'Carolan (1670-1738). Since his death, 220 of his works have been collected and published. The influence of Italian baroque composition is evident in the piece known as *Carolan's Concerto*. The destruction of the Irish nobility in the 17th century removed the social conditions upon which the poet-musicians such as Carolan had, from the earliest times, relied for patronage.

In the 18th century, Dublin became an important centre of music attracting such composers as Geminiani, Arne and Händel.

An Irishman with considerable influence on Romantic composers from Chopin to Glinka was John Field (1782-1837), creator of the nocturne and one of the foremost pianists of his day. Two of the Irish composers of the 19th century who achieved distinction through their operas were Michael Balfe (1808-70), whose best-known composition was *The Bohemian Girl*, and Vincent Wallace (1812-65) who composed *Maritana*. Charles Villiers Stanford (1852-1924) and Hamilton Harty (1879-1941) were also highly regarded.

Most contemporary Irish composers have been influenced by their studies in European schools but the corpus of new musical composition represents a variety of highly individual if related styles.

Well-known composers are Aloys Fleischmann (1910-   ), Frederick May (1911-   ), Brian Boydell (1917-   ), AJ Potter (1918-80), Gerard Victory (1921-   ), Seán Ó Riada (1931-71), John Kinsella (1932-   ), Seoirse Bodley (1933-   ), John Purser (1942-   ) and Frank Corcoran (1944-   ).

Music

Radio Telefís Éireann, which maintains two orchestras as well as a small choir and a string quartet, is the backbone of professional musical performance in Ireland. The RTE Symphony Orchestra has been the platform for the launching of most modern Irish composition. Other orchestras include the Cork Symphony Orchestra, the New Irish Chamber Orchestra and the Irish Youth Orchestra.

The Dublin Grand Opera Society presents two seasons of opera in Dublin annually, one of which is usually transferred to Cork. The Irish National Opera brings opera to other cities and towns in Ireland. The Wexford Opera Festival, a twelve-day event at the end of October, has achieved a major international reputation. There are a number of other music festivals in Ireland which attract participants of many nationalities, including the Waterford Festival of Light Opera and the Cork Choral and Folk Dance Festival, held in the Spring.

In 1974 the Government financed the establishment of the Irish Ballet Company, based in Cork, where there has been a ballet company in existence since 1934.

Music is encouraged in schools by the Department of Education, both by including it as a subject in the syllabuses and promoting live performances in the class-rooms. The Music Association of Ireland operates a schools recital scheme, with programmes by professional artists and ensembles. Musical education is also provided by the Royal Irish Academy of Music, the College of Music in Dublin, and the Cork and Limerick Municipal Schools of Music. Academic teaching is provided by University College, Dublin, Queen's University, Belfast, University College, Cork, and Trinity College, Dublin (where music was first taught in 1612). There are a number of festivals for young people. The *Feis Cheoil*, held in Dublin in early May, is the most important. The late Count John McCormack is probably its most distinguished prizewinner, but the *Feis* has been the springboard for a great deal of Irish musical talent in this century.

148
149

150
151

152
153

154
155

156

157

Music

Ireland is unique among the countries of western Europe in the richness and vitality of its folk music, both vocal and instrumental. This music is still one of the most popular forms of music in Ireland today. A number of festivals of Irish music *(fleadh cheoil)* take place in various centres in Ireland each year.

Traditional vocal music includes English and Scottish ballads imported centuries ago, Anglo-Irish songs and ballads dating mostly from the 19th and early 20th centuries and, above all, the forms of singing Irish in the old style or *sean-nós.* Singing is usually solo where the music relies on the melody ornamented by melismatic, rhythmic and intervallic variation. A great many of such songs have been collected by the Irish Folklore Commission (now the Department of Folklore at University College, Dublin). Instrumental music is played on instruments such as the fiddle, tin whistle, wooden concert flute and *uilleann* pipes and includes dances such as jigs, reels, hornpipes, slides and polkas as well as slow airs based on the vocal music. The Department of Education is at present compiling a complete collection of the dance music and a major cataloguing venture is in progress at University College, Cork.

In recent years, largely under the influence of Seán Ó Riada (1931-71), some musicians have begun to treat their material in new and exciting ways while remaining faithful to the tradition. The new function thus provided for the music has infused fresh vitality into it. The wider acceptance achieved for it is not confined to Ireland — Irish traditional music is attracting increasing attention abroad.

Science

A number of scientific advances of seminal importance have been the work of Irishmen. The 17th-century physicist, Robert Boyle (1627-91) contributed Boyle's Law. William Rowan Hamilton (1805-65) invented quaternion calculus and made important contributions in the fields of optics and dynamics. More recently advances in research have been made by GF Fitzgerald (1851-1901) (Fitzgerald-Lorentz contraction), PLJ Nolan and LW Pollack (photo-electric nucleus counter), Nobel prizewinner ETS Walton (transmutation of the atomic nucleus), JC Synge (theoretical physics), and EJ Conway (biochemistry).

Before 1940, research in Ireland tended to be on a small scale, mainly carried on by a limited number of specialists each supported by a few assistants. The subsequent period has seen major advances in Irish science with increased facilities in the universities and the establishment of new research institutes.

In 1967, the Government, acting on the recommendations of the OECD, set up the National Science Council to advise it on national policies for research, development and technology. The Council was reconstituted in 1978 as the National Board for Science and Technology with wider powers.

Scientific research is carried on in all the universities and equivalent third-level institutions, the major sources of funds being the Higher Education Authority, the National Board for Science and Technology and the Medical Research Council, with some funds coming from other Irish sources and from abroad.

The Dublin Institute of Advanced Studies (founded by the State in 1940) has, in addition to its School of Celtic Studies, two scientific schools, the School of Theoretical Physics and the School of Cosmic Physics. The Institute commissions the writing of scholarly works, trains advanced students in methods of original research and provides academics

Science

159. Geological · sampling at mine workings by IIRS technicians.

160. Furniture testing, using a special-purpose rig at the IIRS test laboratory.

with facilities for advanced study and research.

Since its foundation in 1785, the Royal Irish Academy has promoted the study of science. It assists research in the natural sciences and the humanities, publishes learned papers, and is the body through which Ireland adheres to international scientific unions. The Royal Dublin Society (founded in 1731) maintains a scientific library and publishes a learned journal.

The following are the main specialised research organisations in Ireland, largely funded by the State:

■ *An Foras Talúntais*, the Agricultural Institute, (1958) is the largest research institute in the State and undertakes research over a wide spectrum of agricultural disciplines. It has over 20 research centres in various parts of the country.

■ The Institute for Industrial Research and Standards (IIRS) (1946) assists the growth and development of Irish industry by providing the necessary scientific and technological support and by the identification and provision of new technological investment opportunities.

■ The Economic and Social Research Institute (1961) was established to improve facilities for carrying out economic and social research in the country and in particular to work on problems related to the development of the Irish economy.

■ *An Foras Forbartha*, the National Institute for Physical Planning and Construction Research, (1964) undertakes general research in physical planning and development, building and construction, and roads and water resources.

Some Government Departments have developed large internal research programmes. These include the Department of Agriculture (veterinary and cereal research), the Department of Fisheries and Forestry

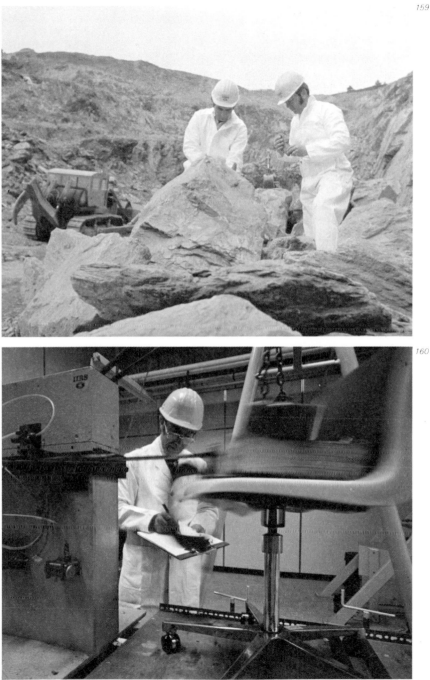

Science

161. Water sampling in a study of an estuary designated as a site for major industry.

162. The testing of a natural gas pipe at the IIRS building laboratory.

(breeding and fisheries research, forestry and wildlife research) and the Department of Industry and Energy. The Industrial Development Authority (IDA) operates an industrial research grants scheme.

In the private sector many industrial firms conduct programmes of research and development, especially in the electrical and electronic, chemical and engineering fields.

Ireland is playing an increasing role in international scientific activities, such as those of the European Communities, the International Atomic Energy Agency, the European Science Foundation, the OECD and the European Space Agency.

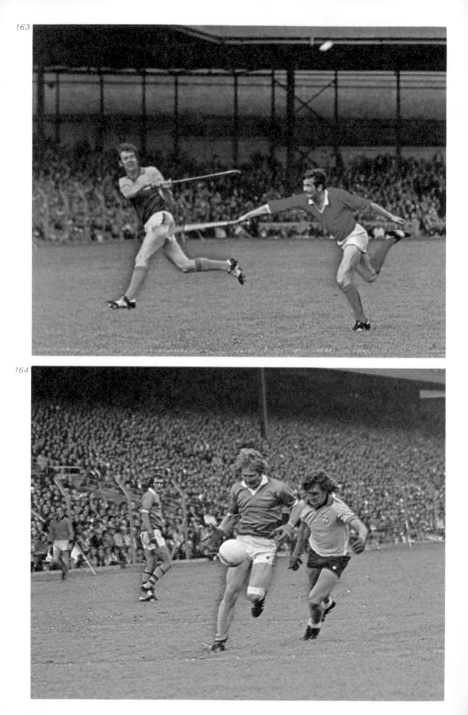

163. Wexford (gold and purple jerseys) opposed Cork (red jerseys) in the 1977 All-Ireland Hurling Final at Croke Park in September 1977. On that occasion, Cork created a new record in winning the title for the 23rd time.

164. Dublin (blue jerseys), a team which rose from obscurity to become the outstanding Gaelic football team of the 1970s, is seen here playing one of the game's most successful teams, Kerry (green jerseys with gold band) in the 1976 All-Ireland Final at Croke Park. Dublin won the title that year but Kerry took the title for the following four years.

Sport

Favoured by the mild climate which permits year-round play in most games, upwards of 60 sports are provided for through various national governing bodies, most of which receive Government aid.

The most popular amateur field games in Ireland are Gaelic football and hurling, traditional games of great antiquity now played according to rules established by the Gaelic Athletic Association (GAA) which organises and administers these sports. The GAA was founded in 1884 and is the largest amateur sports organisation in Ireland. Games are organised through local clubs and county teams. Championship matches are played between county teams each year leading to an All-Ireland final in each game at Croke Park, Dublin, in September. The finals attract crowds of up to 70,000.

Hurling is a game of great skill, considered the fastest field game in the world. It is played on a grass surface by two teams of fifteen players each. The teams contest for possession of a small leather ball with hurley sticks about one metre long. While a large degree of legitimate body contact is allowed, technical expertise is more important than brawn. Camogie is a women's game based on hurling.

Gaelic football has elements in common with both rugby and Association football but is most closely related to the Australian Rules game (derived from it), with which it shares such characteristics as high-catching of the ball, body-charging and fielding the ball in flight or on the hop.

Other popular traditional games include handball. A peculiar aspect of the game as played in Ireland is the use of a hard ball, which results in extremely fast play.

Bowling is especially popular in some areas, such as Cork and Armagh. Played on open roads, a long bowl shot with a twelve-kilo steel ball on a flat road can exceed 200 metres.

165. Greyhound racing.

166. Eddie Macken on Boomerang at the RDS, Dublin.

167. Sailing off Dún Laoghaire, Co. Dublin.

168. Fishing.

169. Racing at the Curragh, one of Ireland's most modern racecourses. It is also the headquarters of the Irish Turf Club. About 1,500 horses, trained on the plains of the Curragh, are stabled in the area.

170. Handball at Croke Park, Dublin. This court, which has 3 glass walls was specially constructed for the World Championship held in Ireland in 1970, an event which provided a major stimulus to the revival of handball.

171. Road bowling at Clonakilty, Co. Cork.

172. The fifth hole of Killarney's golf course.

Sport

Association football (soccer) has become increasingly popular in recent years, while rugby, golf, tennis and other racket games are well supported. The Irish Rugby Football Union celebrated its centenary in 1974.

Because of Ireland's favourable geographical position, there are ample facilities for sea-fishing in coastal waters for the northern cold-water species as well as for warm-water species in the summer and autumn. The abundance of fresh-water fish in Ireland's largely unpolluted rivers and lakes and the access to free fishing account for the popularity of angling in Ireland, particularly with visitors. Other water-based sports such as sailing, surfing, swimming, sub-aqua and water skiing, thrive in congenial conditions.

Horse breeding and racing have always been a major activity in Ireland. The Turf Club, established in the 18th century, controls equestrian sport. In 1945, the Government set up the Racing Board, to develop the competitiveness of racing, nationally and internationally, by increasing the stake money and prizes at horse races, up-grading race-courses and amenities, improving breeding and developing the export trade in horses. Today Ireland disburses some of the highest prizes in world racing. There are twenty-eight race-courses in the country providing about 250 days of racing each year.

Irish thoroughbred horses are among the finest in the world. Major bloodstock sales such as those held at Kill, Co. Kildare and Ballsbridge, Dublin, attract many foreign buyers.

Ireland is a major world centre for the breeding and sale of greyhounds. A Government agency, *Bord na gCon*, controls the promotion and operation of greyhound track racing and the export of greyhounds. It also has overall control of coursing.

Economy

Living Standards

There are over 850,000 private households in Ireland with an average number of persons per household close to four. A remarkably high proportion of householders own their own houses or are in the process of buying them with mortgages. Less than 30% of households are in rented accommodation and only around 13% are rented from private landlords.

About 95% of all households have television sets and over half the households in the country have a car. Some 85% of households own a refrigerator and 65% a washing machine. The incidence of telephones in households is lower at 34% although a substantial investment programme is underway to increase the number of connections.

Per capita consumption of foodstuffs in Ireland is quite high and significant changes have taken place in recent years in the composition of food consumption. There has been a substantial increase in the consumption of beef, pigmeat and cheese while the consumption of eggs, potatoes and, to a lesser extent, dairy products has fallen.

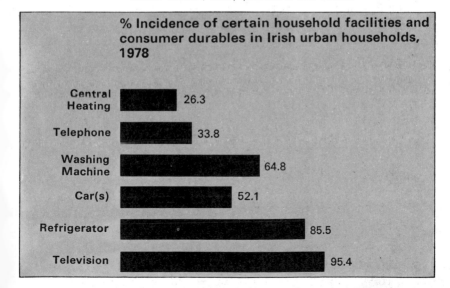

% Incidence of certain household facilities and consumer durables in Irish urban households, 1978

Central Heating	26.3
Telephone	33.8
Washing Machine	64.8
Car(s)	52.1
Refrigerator	85.5
Television	95.4

Economic Development

The increased pace of economic development since the 1960s has been accompanied by significant changes in the composition of output and employment. In 1980 employment in industry (including construction) accounted for over 32% of total employment, compared to about 21% in 1949, while agricultural employment represented less than 21% of total employment, compared to 43% in 1949.

Perhaps the most profound structural change which has taken place in Ireland since the mid-1960s has been the sustained increase in population. The rate of natural increase is high, averaging 1.1% between 1971 and 1979, and this reflects the increased marriage rate and lower marriage age associated with improved economic prosperity. The drain on population through emigration which began in the middle of the last century has ceased. Net emigration, which averaged over 13,000 in each year of the 1960s, gave way to net immigration of a similar magnitude in the 1970s. The population was nearly 3.4 million in 1979 compared with less than 3 million in 1971, an annual average increase of 1.5%. None of the other EEC countries is likely to experience population increase at a similar rate. These demographic changes have fundamental implications for long-term planning in housing and education, social and medical services and, most importantly, in employment needs.

In addition to the number of jobs which must be created to provide for the expected increase in the labour force, the high level of unemployment must be reduced and provision made for the expected continued outflow from agriculture. The Government's strategy for employment expansion is largely based on industrial development which is actively promoted by specialised Government agencies. An attractive range of incentives is available to encourage the establishment of new industries — both foreign and domestic. In determining the aid package for new development, preference is given to industries with strong growth potential, a high value-added content, and the capacity to use indigenous resources.

The Government recognises that, because of the need to expand employment, further development of the economy is an urgent necessity. To provide the basis for this, priority will continue to be given to the improvement and extension of the national infrastructure. Economic and social planning will also be given a high priority and the main objective of this planning process will be to achieve economic and financial stability which is a prerequisite to genuine social and economic development.

The appointment in 1981 of a Minister of State with special responsibility for economic and social planning, together with the proposed establishment of a National Planning Board are intended to give fresh impetus to the planning process in Government policy.

Sectoral distribution of employment, 1980

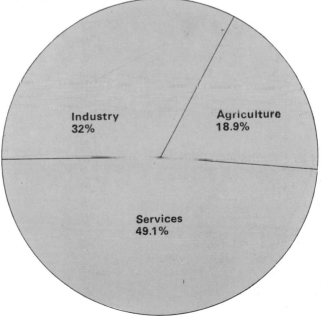

Industry 32%

Agriculture 18.9%

Services 49.1%

Agriculture

Above, the symbol of the National Dairy Council, the function of which is to promote increased consumption of milk and Irish dairy products on the home market.

174. A herd of Friesian cattle at Lough Egish, Co. Cavan.

Employment

In spite of the relatively faster growth of other sectors since the Second World War, agriculture remains a very important source of output and employment in Ireland. Productivity growth in the industry has been high but this has been due to a fairly rapid fall in employment and substantial increases in output. The main reductions in farm employment have been due to decreases in the number of relatives assisting on farms, who now account for less than 20% of farm employment compared to 33% in 1951, and in those employed by farmers, who represented 16% of the agricultural labour force in 1951 compared to less than 10% at present. The smallest decline was experienced by farmers, almost all of whom are owner-occupiers.

Land Tenure

The pattern of agricultural land tenure is based on owner-proprietorship achieved by way of State purchase of former landlords' interests through the agency of the Land Commission. The improvement of land structure through the acquisition and division of land and the re-arrangement of intermixed holdings is now the main task of the Land Commission. The average size of agricultural holdings in Ireland is not large, though it is comparable with the size of holdings in most other EEC member countries. Over 90% of agricultural land in Ireland is under grass and this reflects the importance of livestock production in Irish agriculture.

Output

Some 85% of the value of gross output in agriculture is accounted for by livestock and livestock products. Cattle and calves represent about three-quarters of livestock production. Pigs, sheep and lambs account for most of the remainder. Milk and butter production accounts for over 90% of the output of livestock products.

Although crop production represents only about 13% of output, the production of barley, wheat,

Agriculture

175. A flock of sheep grazing.

176. Charolais cattle at the RDS Spring Show in Dublin.

177. Galtee cheese being produced at the Mitchelstown Co-operative in Co. Cork. Many of the larger modern amalgamated dairy co-operatives have daily capacities in the region of 500,000 gallons, with annual turnover of IR£50 million to IR£100 million.

178. Harvesting.

sugar beet and potatoes represents an important source of farm income.

While many farms have a mixed output combining a small acreage devoted to tillage and a much larger area devoted to pasture there are substantial regional variations. In the midlands, east and south, the land is excellent, farm sizes are larger and average incomes higher. In the midlands fat cattle production is particularly important and large numbers of store cattle are moved there from other parts of the country for finishing. In the south, dairy farming is predominant while, in the south-east, intensive mixed farming is carried on with substantial production of sugar beet, barley and wheat. In the poorer, and generally smaller, holdings in the west, farmers engage in mixed farming, often including sheep production, and many of them supplement their incomes by other activities.

Exports

Ireland has traditionally been a net exporter of agricultural products and goods based on agricultural products. Over half of the value of agricultural production is exported. However, for cattle and beef production the export proportion is higher with about 80% of disposals going abroad. An increasing proportion of agricultural output is undergoing processing before export. For example, live exports of cattle and calves now account for only about 30% of cattle and beef exports, compared to over 60% in the mid-1960s.

EEC

Membership of the European Communities has benefited Irish agriculture in a number of ways. The Common Agricultural Policy has ensured better prices for producers and given Irish farmers access to an extensive market for their output. Assistance from European Community resources is also available for certain schemes designed to effect structural improvements in agriculture. As well as making a domestic contribution to the EEC

development and restructuring schemes, the State provides an extensive disease eradication scheme for farmers and supports a widely used agricultural advisory service.

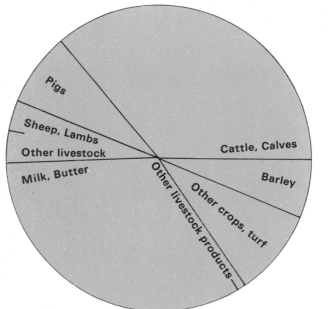

Distribution of farm output, 1979

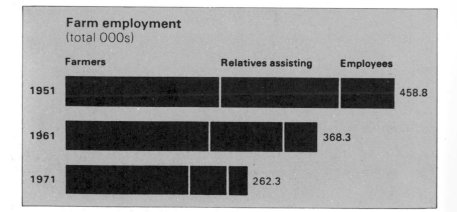

Farm employment
(total 000s)

	Farmers	Relatives assisting	Employees	
1951				458.8
1961				368.3
1971				262.3

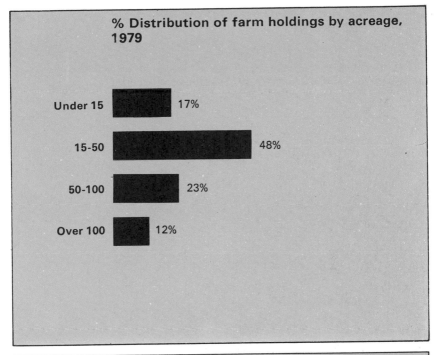

% Distribution of farm holdings by acreage, 1979

- Under 15 — 17%
- 15-50 — 48%
- 50-100 — 23%
- Over 100 — 12%

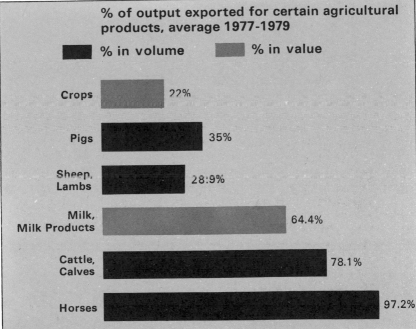

% of output exported for certain agricultural products, average 1977-1979

- % in volume
- % in value

- Crops — 22%
- Pigs — 35%
- Sheep, Lambs — 28:9%
- Milk, Milk Products — 64.4%
- Cattle, Calves — 78.1%
- Horses — 97.2%

Forestry

In 1920, the area under woodland in Ireland was
less than 1% of the total land area. This low level of
afforestation was a result of clearances for
agriculture and the pressures of demand for fuel
from industry — iron smelting in particular. Since the
foundation of the State, vigorous efforts to increase
the area under forest have been made. There are
now over 293,000 hectares of State plantation. The
annual planting target is 10,000 hectares. This
State programme employs about 2,700 people. In
addition private planting is encouraged through
grants and a free advisory service. At present about
5% of total land area is under woodland. In recent
years the State has developed many forest areas to
provide facilities for public recreation.

Fisheries

Sea Fishing

Many species of fish are found in the seas off Ireland's extensive coastline. The main varieties landed are herring, cod, whiting, mackerel, plaice, ray, skate and haddock. Among shell-fish, lobsters, periwinkles, crayfish and oysters are taken. For a long time the stock of fish around Ireland's shores was a relatively neglected natural resource. However in recent years a major development programme has been underway.

Bord Iascaigh Mhara (Sea Fisheries Board) is the State body with responsibility for the development of the sea fishing industry. The Board provides financial assistance towards investment in vessels, assistance in the development of home and export markets and educational and advisory services for fishermen. In 1979, the total value of the catch (including salmon), as landed by Irish registered vessels in Irish ports, was IR£30.1 million, while exports of fish and fish products were valued at IR£33.2 million. About 3,300 full-time and 5,400 part-time fishermen are employed in the industry.

Inland Fisheries

The most important species of fish in Irish inland waters is the Atlantic salmon. In 1979 the value of landings of salmon amounted to IR£5.2 million and exports to IR£3.9 million. The fishery provides seasonal employment for about 6,000 men. Eel fishing is also important, exports being valued at about IR£392,000 in 1979.

In addition to the commercial value of inland fisheries, salmon, brown-trout and sea-trout angling on the many Irish rivers and lakes provides excellent sport for Irish and foreign anglers and contributed approximately IR£18 million in 1979 to earnings from tourism. In recent years sea-angling and angling for coarse fish such as pike, perch, bream, rudd, tench and carp have become very popular and are also attracting visiting anglers in increasing numbers.

181. Construction
work in progress at
Killala, Co. Mayo on
the Asahi Chemical
International textile
plant.

182. AW Faber
Castell (Ireland) Ltd
which manufactures
pencils, ball-point
pens, fibre and felt-
tip writers at Fermoy,
Co. Cork.

Industry

When independence was achieved, the industrial
sector accounted for only about one-eighth of total
employment. In the 1930s, however, the imposition
of relatively high tariff barriers led to the development
of many new industries, small in scale and catering
almost exclusively for the home market. In the
1950s, it was recognised that the opportunities for
expanding employment further through dependence
on the domestic market were limited and increased
emphasis was laid on encouraging export expansion.
Capital grants for new export industries were
introduced and tax concessions on profits from
exports were granted. A major effort to attract
foreign enterprise was commenced and existing
industries were aided in improving their efficiency so
as to withstand free trade. In 1965, the Anglo-Irish
Free Trade Area Agreement was signed and by
1975 virtually all tariffs on imports from the United
Kingdom had been abolished. Irish membership of
the EEC from 1 January 1973 has led to a gradual
reduction in tariffs on imports from other EEC
member-countries and by 1978 practically all trade
between Ireland and the rest of the EEC became
tariff-free.

Industrial expansion has been a major source of
growth in the Irish economy over the past decade.
The average annual rate of growth of manufactured
output between 1965 and 1978 was 5.7%. The
fastest growing industries over this period included
chemicals, textiles, clay products, metals,
engineering and food.

Much of the expansion in manufacturing industry has
come from the attraction of a large number of
foreign-based firms to Ireland. The Industrial
Development Authority has statutory responsibility for
industrial development in Ireland. The Authority
provides an attractive and comprehensive package of
incentives for industrialists abroad who are interested
in establishing new industries in Ireland as well as
assisting the expansion and re-equipment of existing
Irish industry. The range of incentives includes non-

Industry

183. Glass crystal was made in Waterford from 1783 to 1851. 100 years later, a new factory opened there and Waterford Glass Ltd now employs well over 2,000 persons in the production of its world-renowned lead crystal and soda lime glass.

184. Technicon (Ireland) Ltd, a subsidiary of Technicon Instruments Corp., USA, has been producing instruments for automatic chemical analysis since 1966.

repayable grants towards the cost of fixed asset investment, provision of ready-built factories, provision of housing for key workers, payment of training grants and loan guarantees. The Authority, from its inception, has provided over IR£2,550 million of investment in fixed assets and entered grant commitments of over IR£737 million. The countries of origin for externally promoted projects include the United States, the United Kingdom, the Federal Republic of Germany, the Netherlands and Japan. The new industries attracted by the Authority cover a wide spectrum of activities including chemicals, textiles, pharmaceuticals, engineering, electronics and food processing.

Údaras na Gaeltachta (the Gaeltacht Authority), is the Government agency with sole responsibility for industrial development in the *Gaeltacht* (Irish-speaking areas in the west of Ireland). The *Gaeltacht* is designated by the Government as a top priority area for development. Consequently, the Authority is empowered to offer valuable incentives and assistance to industries setting up in the *Gaeltacht*, including capital grants, training costs, advance factories at subsidised rentals and a wide range of advisory and assistance services. The Authority is also actively involved in the management of over 40 companies in which it has a shareholding.

Over 45% of the gross output of Irish industry is now exported, compared to 20% in 1961. From 1970 to 1978 exports in the chemical/pharmaceutical sector increased from IR£14 million to IR£331 million. The volume growth rate of this sector in the same period was the highest reached in all OECD countries. In 1978, 69% of the textile industry's production was exported.

A substantial proportion of industrial activity takes place in the east coast region — comprising Dublin and the surrounding counties — which accounts for almost half of total industrial employment and over half of manufacturing employment. In the context of

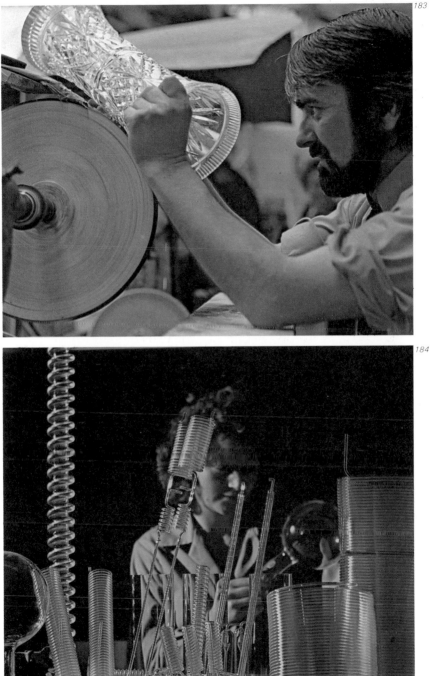

185

186

185. Irish Distillers
Ltd is the holding
company formed for
the merger of the
major Irish distillery
concerns, Powers,
Jameson, Cork
Distillers and
Bushmills. It markets
and exports whiskey,
gin, vodka and white
rum.

186. Electric cable
being manufactured
at Irish Cable and
Wire, an Irish firm
established at
Athlone, Co.
Westmeath in
1972.

187. Smelting at the
Irish Steel plant,
Haulbowline, Cobh,
Co. Cork. Irish Steel
is State-owned and
supplies a sizeable
proportion of all steel
in Ireland.

Industry

188. Killarney Hosiery Co. Ltd, a subsidiary of the British firm, Pretty Polly Ltd. The plant commenced operations in 1967.

189. Henry Ford and Son Ltd has been in production at Marina, Cork, for over half a century.

its development policy the Industrial Development Authority is attempting to obtain a more even spread of industrial employment and special concessions are available to industries which are located in peripheral and less developed areas. The Shannon Free Airport Development Company manages an industrial estate at Shannon Airport, the world's first customs-free airport.

The inflow of foreign industrial enterprises combined with the modernisation and expansion of existing Irish industry has increased the need for skilled personnel. A major rôle in the training of industrial workers is played by AnCO — the Industrial Training Authority. This State agency, which was established in 1967, promotes training schemes in industry and provides facilities in industrial training centres for the training of unemployed and redundant workers and for the initial training of apprentices. The Authority is financed by a levy on employers (which is repayable if an approved training scheme is in operation), by central Government funds and by grants from the EEC Social Fund.

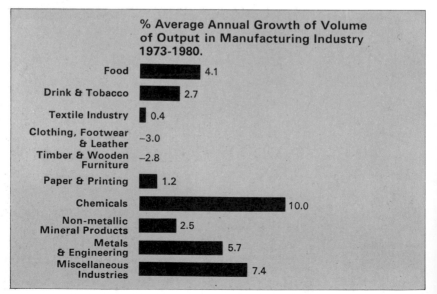

% Average Annual Growth of Volume of Output in Manufacturing Industry 1973-1980.

Food	4.1
Drink & Tobacco	2.7
Textile Industry	0.4
Clothing, Footwear & Leather	−3.0
Timber & Wooden Furniture	−2.8
Paper & Printing	1.2
Chemicals	10.0
Non-metallic Mineral Products	2.5
Metals & Engineering	5.7
Miscellaneous Industries	7.4

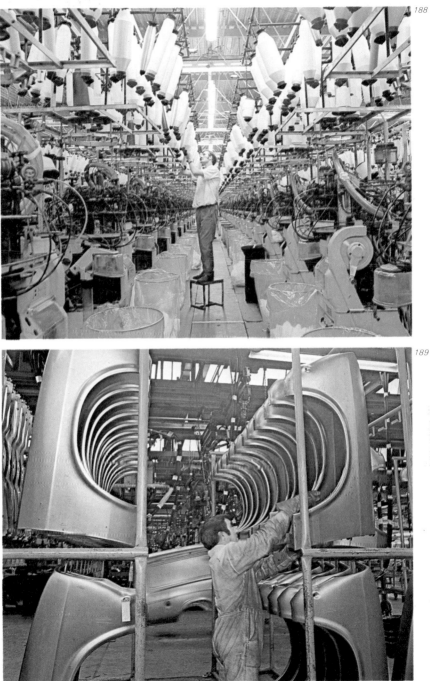

Mining

The notable revival in mineral exploration since 1960 which led to the discovery and development of several valuable mineral deposits received an added impetus with the discovery in 1970 of the large zinc/lead deposit at Navan, Co. Meath. This deposit came into production in 1977. Ireland, currently ranking as a leading European producer of baryte and lead-zinc ores with a high silver content, will, at the full production of the mine, become a leading world producer of zinc ores. Ireland also has considerable outputs of copper and sulphur ores, gypsum, dolomite, limestone flour and aggregates, as well as smaller outputs of coal and of green and black marble. There is no slackening of interest in exploration. Prospecting licences are issued by the Minister for Industry and Energy subject to certain conditions and normally for a maximum of six years.

Mining

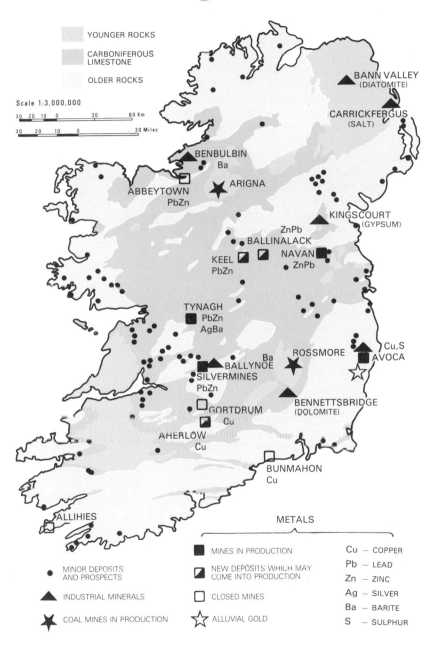

YOUNGER ROCKS

CARBONIFEROUS LIMESTONE

OLDER ROCKS

Scale 1:3,000,000

30 20 10 0 30 60 Km

30 20 10 0 30 Miles

BANN VALLEY (DIATOMITE)

CARRICKFERGUS (SALT)

BENBULBIN
Ba

ABBEYTOWN
PbZn

ARIGNA

KINGSCOURT (GYPSUM)

ZnPb
BALLINALACK

KEEL
PbZn

NAVAN
ZnPb

TYNAGH
PbZn
AgBa

Ba
ROSSMORE

Cu,S
AVOCA

BALLYNOE
SILVERMINES
PbZn

GORTDRUM
Cu

BENNETTSBRIDGE (DOLOMITE)

AHERLOW
Cu

BUNMAHON
Cu

ALLIHIES

METALS

● MINOR DEPOSITS AND PROSPECTS

▲ INDUSTRIAL MINERALS

★ COAL MINES IN PRODUCTION

■ MINES IN PRODUCTION

◪ NEW DEPOSITS WHICH MAY COME INTO PRODUCTION

☐ CLOSED MINES

☆ ALLUVIAL GOLD

Cu — COPPER

Pb — LEAD

Zn — ZINC

Ag — SILVER

Ba — BARITE

S — SULPHUR

Industrial Relations

Trade unionism first emerged in the largest cities (Dublin, Belfast and Cork) during the 18th century despite legislation against combination of workers. This development continued in the 19th century and a number of British unions also established branches in Ireland.

The first association of trade unions, representing thirty crafts and industries, was formed in 1863 and in 1894 the Irish Trade Unions Congress representing most Irish and a number of British unions was established.

The Irish Congress of Trade Unions (ICTU), which is the main co-ordinating body for Irish unions, including unions in Northern Ireland, was set up in 1959. At present 68 unions representing 429,000 workers are affiliated to the ICTU.

There are 132 trade unions operating in Ireland. Of these, 96 are workers' unions and the remainder employers' unions.

A union based outside Ireland may operate in Ireland provided it has a controlling authority resident in Ireland which is empowered to make decisions of a political and economic nature in relation to the Irish membership of the union. There are at present 16 foreign-based unions operating in Ireland.

The Irish Transport and General Workers' Union is the largest union with 166,000 members. Other large unions are the Federated Workers' Union of Ireland (47,000 members) and the Amalgamated Transport and General Workers' Union (25,000 members).

The representative organisation of the management side of industry and business is the Federated Union of Employers (FUE). There are also a number of other employers' associations which are organised on a craft or regional basis.

In 1970, the Employer-Labour Conference, a

Industrial Relations

voluntary body which provides equal representation for employers and trade unions under an independent chairman, was established to provide a national forum for the discussion and review of developments in money incomes and prices. Between 1970 and 1978 the Conference negotiated seven successive National Wage Agreements. In 1979 and 1980, the National Understandings, which replaced the National Wage Agreements, and which cover such matters as employment, taxation, social welfare and health in addition to pay and industrial relations, gave an important role to the Employer-Labour Conference in relation to pay policy. Wages and other conditions of employment are, in general, matters for settlement by free collective bargaining.

The Labour Court, an independent body established in 1946, provides machinery for the formal investigation of disputes between employers and workers. The Chairman and Deputy Chairmen of the Court are appointed by the Minister for Labour and four members each are nominated by the FUE and the ICTU. When a dispute is referred to the Court by either the trade unions or the employers or both, the Court normally appoints an Industrial Relations Officer to mediate in the dispute through conciliation conferences. If conciliation fails, it is open to the parties to request a formal investigation by the Court.

For certain industries and trades, Joint Labour Committees operate. They propose minimum rates of pay and other conditions of employment which are legally binding when ratified by the Court in the form of Employment Regulation Orders. The Court may register employment agreements relating to the remuneration or the conditions of employment of certain workers. A registered employment agreement is binding on the employer and on every worker of the class, type or group to which it is expressed to apply. The Court also registers voluntary bodies known as Joint Industrial Councils which provide a forum for the negotiation of issues arising within particular industries or parts of industries.

192

193

194

192. A Bord na Móna peat-harvesting machine.

193. The Allenwood peat fired electricity generating station.

194. The gas-fired electricity generating station at Aghada, Co. Cork while under construction.

Energy

Although Ireland lacks sizeable coal deposits, it has a valuable energy source in the peat or turf bogs which cover parts of the Central Plain and large areas along the west, south and north-west coasts. Traditionally peat has been cut by hand from the bog and used as a domestic fuel. *Bord na Móna* (the Peat Board), a State-sponsored body, has now turned it into a valuable and efficient source of domestic and industrial power. Peat is used to generate a considerable proportion of the total production of electricity and in the form of machine turf and briquettes makes a substantial contribution to the solid fuel market. Moss peat is also used extensively in horticultural activities. The recent sharp increases in energy prices have greatly increased the value of Ireland's peat resources and *Bord na Móna* is at present engaged in a major expansion programme. The Board's engineers have also developed sophisticated machines to harvest peat from the bogs. In 1978/79, *Bord na Móna* employed a peak of 6,255 workers and produced about 4 million tons of fuel peat (the thermal equivalent of over 978,000 tonnes of oil) and over 1 million cubic metres of moss peat.

Statutory responsibility for the generation and distribution of electricity is vested in the Electricity Supply Board, established by the State in 1927. The Board has over 1 million customers many of whom live in rural areas where the Rural Electrification Scheme has brought electricity to virtually all homes in the state. The domestic distribution system operates at 220 volts/50 cycles.

Present output of electricity is about 8,500 million units. About 11,900 people are employed in the industry and the Board is engaged in a substantial plant expansion programme. Domestic demand represents about 42% of sales while the balance is used by industrial and commercial concerns.

About 64% of the total fuel required for electricity generation is provided from imported fuel oil and the remainder from domestic energy sources, with peat

Energy

accounting for about 16% of fuel requirements and hydro, gas and coal stations providing the remainder.

Since the late 1960s, there has been considerable interest in exploration for gas and oil in the Continental Shelf that surrounds Ireland. In August 1973, a commercial gasfield was discovered sould of Kinsale Head which is estimated to contain reserves of approximately 1.35 million million cubic feet of high quality natural gas capable of sustaining an output of at least 125 million cubic feet of gas per day for 20 years. The field went into production in 1978 and the output will be used to generate up to 510 megawatts of electricity for the Electricity Supply Board in the Marina and Aghada power stations in Cork. The Aghada power station is expected to commence operations in 1981. Kinsale gas is also used to provide a feedstock for the production of fertilisers by the State-sponsored fertiliser company *Nítrigin Éireann Teo.* (Nitrogen Ireland Ltd), and will in the future provide domestic gas supplies in the Cork city region. An allocation of gas has also been made available to various industrial users in the area including Irish Steel Ltd.

Other wells drilled have produced 'shows' of oil of significant magnitude but further drilling is required to establish the presence of commercially viable reserves. In 1976, a number of petroleum exploration licences were granted to petroleum industry consortia in respect of exploration in the offshore areas of Ireland. The areas covered include blocks in the south-west, west, north-west and east. A wide-ranging drilling programme in the Continental Shelf area will be underway by the mid-1980s.

195. The upper reservoir and lower lake at Lough Nahangan, which provide the water for the ESB's pumped-storage electricity generating station at Turlough Hill, Co. Wicklow.

196. Construction of a natural gas pipeline in progress.

197. The ESB restocking a river from a salmon hatchery. The ESB operates Europe's second largest hatchery on the river Shannon.

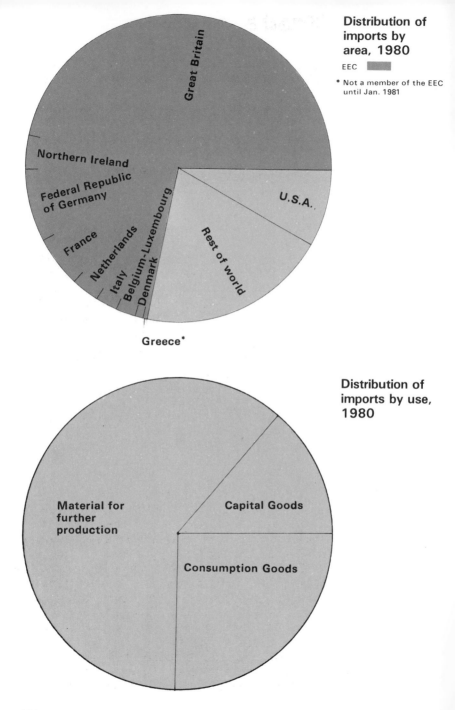

Distribution of imports by area, 1980

EEC

* Not a member of the EEC until Jan. 1981

Great Britain

Northern Ireland

Federal Republic of Germany

France

Netherlands

Italy

Belgium-Luxembourg

Denmark

Greece*

U.S.A.

Rest of world

Distribution of imports by use, 1980

Material for further production

Capital Goods

Consumption Goods

Trade

Export expansion is the main growth factor in the Irish economy. Exports currently account for about 47% of Gross National Product, a high proportion by international standards. Manufactured goods (excluding food, drink and tobacco) constitute the largest category of Irish exports, amounting to about 57% of their total value, a figure which reflects the growing industrialisation of the economy since the early 1960s. At the same time, exports of food, drink and live animals — the main contributors to agriculture-based and agricultural exports — continue to be of considerable importance. The Common Agricultural Policy of the European Economic Community has given access to an EEC-wide market for Irish agricultural exports at greatly improved prices.

The distribution of Irish exports by area has altered considerably in recent years. While the value of exports going to the UK has continued to increase, the proportion has fallen as Irish exporters have expanded trade with other European economies and markets farther afield. Diversification has been aided by Irish membership of the EEC and manufactured as well as agricultural exports to the Community have grown rapidly. The UK now takes around 46% of total Irish exports and the eight Continental member countries 31%; comparative figures for 1973 are 55% and 21%.

The State organisation for the promotion and development of exports is *Córas Tráchtála* (Irish Export Board), which works in close co-operation with the Department of Foreign Affairs and other organisations involved in export promotion. The Board provides a wide variety of aids and facilities for Irish exporters, together with information and other services for foreign buyers and importers. It has a head office in Dublin and 24 offices throughout the world.

In general, Irish imports of goods are well in excess of visible exports. However, receipts from invisible earnings (such as tourism and income from foreign investments and remittances) tend to close the

Trade

resulting gap in the balance of payments. The increase in investment in Ireland by foreign enterprises in recent years has generated a substantial inflow of capital which has helped to finance much of the imports of machinery and other producers' capital goods.

The value of Ireland's imports is mainly accounted for by industrial demand for investment goods, goods for further processing, raw materials and fuels. Imports from the UK, though showing some decrease over the long term, are substantial, amounting to 50% of the total. The share of the other EEC countries has been rising and now stands at almost 22%. The other main source of imports is the United States, which supplies about 9% of Irish needs.

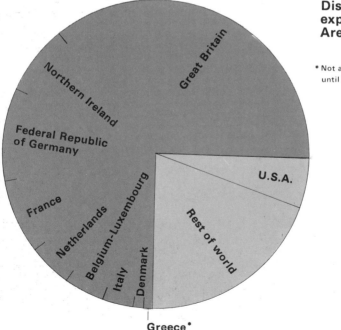

Distribution of exports by Area, 1980

* Not a member of the EEC until Jan. 1981

199

banc ceannais
na h-éireann
1
an gobharnóir
rúnaí na roinne
airgeadais
£1
LLB 144931 10·06·77
LLB 144931

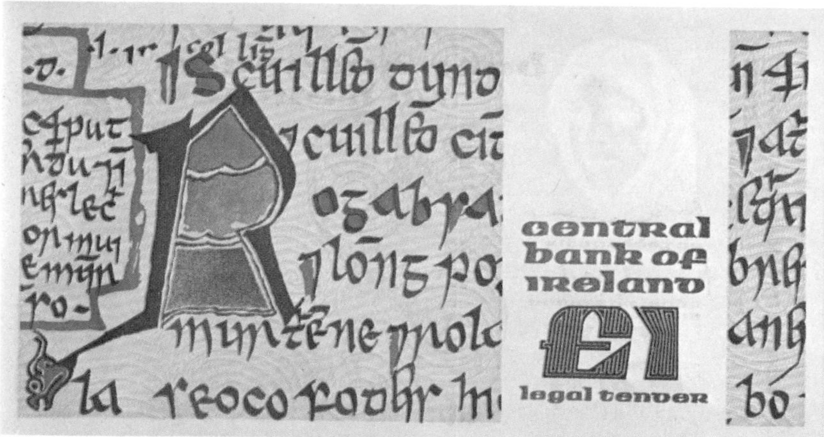
central
bank of
ireland
£1
legal tender

Banking and Currency

The Central Bank of Ireland, established in 1942, is responsible for the formulation and implementation of monetary policy. The bank licenses and supervises the activities of the commercial banks, acts as banker to them, ensures compliance with Ireland's EMS obligations and operates an exchange for the clearance of cheques. It also manages the Government's accounts and the registers of Government stock and acts as custodian of the official external reserves.

There are at present forty-five banks licensed under the terms of the Central Bank Act, 1971. These include the associated banks — Bank of Ireland, Allied Irish Banks Ltd, Northern Bank Ltd and Ulster Bank Ltd — which are the main clearing banks and which provide all general banking services, including current account services. All other licensed banks are known as non-associated banks and fall into four categories — merchant banks, North American banks, industrial banks and other banks. The merchant banks deal mainly in wholesale banking, accepting large deposits and making large loans, and offer a wide range of specialised financial services. While the activities of the North American banks are in some respects similar, these banks compete more fully with the associated banks in providing a full commercial banking service. Industrial banks are primarily engaged in the extension of instalment credit.

The monetary unit is the Irish pound (IR£). Ireland is a participant in the European Monetary Service (EMS). The Central Bank is the sole issuer of currency, with notes issued in the following denominations: IR£1, IR£5, IR£10, IR£20, IR£50 and IR£100. The one pound unit is subdivided into 100 pence (p) with coins ranging from ½p to 50p.

*199. The Irish £1
note (IR£1).*

Tourism

Income from tourism is an important source of foreign earnings for Ireland. Indeed the industry, in terms of export earnings, is more important than any single category of manufacturing industry. While a large number of visitors have links with, or relatives living in, the country, an increasing proportion of those coming to Ireland are tourists in the ordinary sense. They are attracted by the friendliness and hospitality of the people, the variety of the scenery, unspoilt countryside, traffic-free roads and the tranquil way of life.

Visitors from Britain constitute the largest single group both in terms of numbers of arrivals and expenditure. The United States is also an important market, while in recent years there has been a remarkable increase in visitors from EEC countries.

The Irish Tourist Board (Bord Fáilte Éireann) is a statutory organization with a wide range of responsibilities for the promotion and development of the tourist industry. Bord Fáilte marketing activities include market research and planning, direct consumer advertising and promotions in the major market areas. On the development side, the Tourist Board is concerned with the registration and grading of tourist accommodation, the improvement of standards within the tourist industry, the expansion of tourist amenities and alterations generally. The Board is represented in Northern Ireland, Britain, the United States, Canada, Federal Republic of Germany, France, the Netherlands, Belgium, Sweden, Australia, New Zealand and Argentina. At home the Tourist Board co-ordinates the activities of eight Regional Tourism Organizations.

Services

Education

The Irish Constitution recognises that parents are free to provide for the education of their children at home, in private schools or in schools recognised or established by the State. The Department of Education provides education free of charge in primary and second-level schools and it gives substantial aid to universities and other institutions of third-level education.

Primary Schools
Children usually attend school from the age of four years and attendance is compulsory for children between six and fifteen.

Most Irish children attend a State-supported National School. The Department of Education prescribes the educational programme, approves the qualifications and pays the salaries of teachers. It also subjects the schools to regular inspection. Teachers receive their training in Teachers' Training Colleges recognised by the Department of Education but teaching appointments in each school are made by the local management authority. In the school year 1979-80, there were 3,412 National Schools staffed by approximately 19,000 teachers. Approximately 547,500 pupils attended these schools in that year.

In addition to the National Schools, there are over 90 private primary schools, which do not receive State aid.

The local management of the primary schools is entrusted to a board comprising representatives of the parents, the teachers and the appropriate religious authority. The State meets most of the cost of the schools and retains a large measure of control over their operation.

Second-Level Schools
Irish secondary schools, in contrast to the primary schools, are private institutions run by boards of governors, religious communities or individuals, but the Department of Education gives considerable

203. A community
school at Ballincollig,
Co. Cork.

204. Bolton Street
College, one of three
colleges in Dublin
which provide
courses at third level
in certain
technological
disciplines.

Education

assistance by paying a grant in respect of each eligible
pupil. It also pays over 90% of the salaries of
registered teachers employed by the schools. A special
supplemental grant is paid in respect of each eligible
pupil to all schools which do not charge fees and under
this arrrangement all but a very small percentage of
secondary schools offer free education. The
programme of instruction is prescribed by the
Department and the schools are visited regularly by
Departmental inspectors. The ages of secondary
school pupils generally range from twelve to nineteen
years and their school courses last for five to six years.

To qualify for official registration, teachers must be
university graduates who have taken a post-graduate
Diploma in Education, or graduates in art, domestic
science, physical education, woodwork, metalwork
or rural science.

In the school year 1979-80, there were 530
recognised secondary schools, 21 of which
conducted their teaching wholly or partly in Irish. They
had a total of 199,100 pupils and teaching staff
(including part-time teachers) numbered 11,470.

Comprehensive and Community Schools
In addition to secondary schools, there are a number of
post-primary comprehensive and community schools,
which combine academic and practical subjects in a
wide curriculum and provide continuing educational
and vocational guidance for all pupils in their areas.
They thus provide equality of educational opportunity
and offer to each pupil an education structured to his
needs and interests.

In the school year 1979-80, there were 15
Comprehensive Schools with 8,150 pupils and 30
Community Schools with 16,360 pupils. The
number of Comprehensive and Community School
teachers was about 1,545.

Vocational Schools
Parallel to the secondary school system, is a system

Education

of 246 vocational schools which provide pupils who have left primary schools with second-level education and with a general and practical training for employment. These schools also give more specialised technical training for particular trades or professions and provide evening courses for adults in a very wide variety of subjects, ranging from foreign languages through photography and domestic economy to motor-car engineering.

The schools are free of charge. In each county or city they are under the management of a Vocational Educational Committee elected by the local authority for the area. The programmes carried out by the Committees are subject to the control of the Department of Education, which provides approximately nine-tenths of the total cost, the balance being met by the local authority.

Regional Technical Colleges
Regional Technical Colleges have been established in nine provincial centres: Athlone, Carlow, Cork, Dundalk, Galway, Letterkenny, Sligo, Tralee and Waterford. There are also eight Vocational Colleges — five in Dublin, one in Cork, one in Limerick and one in Donegal. The Colleges cater for four main sectors of education: (i) craft apprenticeship and craft-based technician courses; (ii) middle and higher-level technician courses; (iii) professional courses (iv) adult part-time courses.

In the year 1979-80, the attendance at vocational schools, vocational colleges and Regional Technical Colleges totalled 76,380. There were 5,440 teachers at the vocational schools and colleges and 810 at the Regional Technical Colleges.

Examinations
Three post-primary examinations for full-time day pupils are held by the Department each year — the Group Certificate Examination for pupils of 14 or 15 years, the Intermediate Certificate Examination for pupils of 15 or 16 years of age, and the Leaving

Education

Certificate for pupils of 17 or 18 years.

In addition, a series of examinations in art, commercial and trade subjects for adult students and apprentices is held each year.

Universities and Other Third-Level Institutions

There are two universities — the National University of Ireland and Dublin University. The National University was founded in 1908 and comprises three constituent colleges — University College Dublin (UCD) which has over 8,300 full-time students, University College Cork (UCC) with over 4,300 full-time students and University College Galway (UCG) with about 3,600 full-time students. In addition, St Patrick's College, Maynooth, (a seminary for Catholic priests and a Pontifical university with power to confer degrees up to doctoral level in philosophy, theology and canon law) which was founded in 1795, is a 'recognised' college of the National University. It admits lay students to courses in arts, Celtic studies, science and education leading to the award of degrees and diplomas of the National University. It has over 1,000 full-time students, and about 400 students of theology.

Dublin University was established in 1591. It consists of one college — Trinity College, Dublin (TCD) — and has over 5,300 full-time students.

The universities and university colleges are self-governing institutions but they receive a large proportion of their income from the State in the form of annual grants.

The National Institute for Higher Education at Limerick came into operation in 1972. The Institute, which has about 1,250 students, offers mainly technological courses but there is a significant element of the humanities. The first group of students taking diploma courses were awarded diplomas in 1975 and the first group of students

206. The West Front of Trinity College, Dublin viewed from inside Front Square.

207. The Long Room of the Old Library at Trinity College.

208. The Campanile in Front Square, Trinity College.

209. A portion of
the University
College Dublin,
complex, at Belfield.

Education

taking degree courses graduated in 1976. A second
National Institute for Higher Education similar to the
National Institute for Higher Education, Limerick,
opened in Dublin in 1980.

The Thomond College of Education at Limerick trains
teachers specialising in certain areas including
physical education, woodwork, metalwork and rural
science. The first teachers of physical education to
train in the College graduated in 1975.

A National Council for Educational Awards has been
established to validate and award degree and non-
degree third-level qualifications in the non-university
institutions of higher education.

The Higher Education Authority, a statutory body,
advises the Minister for Education and the
Government in regard to the planning of higher
education generally. State grants to the universities
and other designated third-level institutions are
channelled through the Authority.

Medical Education

The medical schools in Ireland are in the constituent
Colleges of the National University at Dublin, Cork
and Galway, in Trinity College, Dublin, and the Royal
College of Surgeons in Ireland, an independent
institution which dates from the 18th century.
Another long-established body in Dublin — the Royal
College of Physicians of Ireland — is empowered to
examine for and award postgraduate (membership
and fellowship) medical qualifications.

KEEP MEDICINES IN PROPORTION

Take your doctor's advice. It's the best medicine!

Health Education Bureau

Health Services

The health services in Ireland are operated by eight
health boards under the general direction of the
Department of Health.

Everyone is entitled to hospital in-patient services as
a public patient, to hospital out-patient services, to
assistance towards the cost of prescriptions and to
subsidised accommodation as a private patient.
However, persons with annual incomes of IR£8,500
or more are liable for consultants' fees as public
patients. Those who are unable to afford general
practitioner services for themselves and their
dependents are entitled to a medical card which
provides them with all medical services, including
drugs and medicines, free of charge. In addition,
persons with annual incomes of less than IR£8,500
are entitled to full maternity services at State
expense. Everyone over the age of sixteen who has
an income is obliged to pay a health contribution of
1% of annual income subject to a maximum of
IR£70. Medical card holders are exempt from this
obligation.

School health examination services, child welfare
clinic services, tuberculosis and infectious diseases
services, in-patient hospital care for children with
certain long-term diseases as well as drugs and
medicines for persons with certain long-term
diseases are available free of charge to all, regardless
of income.

There are schemes which provide for the education,
training for employment and job placement of the
blind and disabled. Cash allowances are also payable
to these in certain circumstances.

A Voluntary Health Insurance Board, established by
the State but with financial autonomy, operates a
voluntary insurance scheme which all may join,
whether or not they are entitled to benefit from the
health services.

Ireland has an excellent system of hospitals — both

Health Services

voluntary and public — which have been assisted for many years by the proceeds of the Irish Hospitals Sweepstakes. There are 5.8 hospital beds per thousand of population, an exceptionally high figure by international standards. The ratios of doctors and dentists — 12.0 and 2.8 per 10,000 of population respectively — also emerge favourably from international comparison.

Medical Research

One of the main bodies in Ireland devoted to medical research is the Medical Research Council of Ireland, which supports research in universities and hospitals and the training of research workers, as well as assisting investigations carried out on public health questions. It has had some striking successes, particularly in the area of clofazimines, used to combat leprosy. The research and development of this drug, which was awarded the UNESCO prize for science in 1981 has been aided by the Development Co-operation Division of the Department of Foreign Affairs as part of Ireland's bilateral aid programme.

The Medico-Social Research Board advises the Minister for Health on and organises research into matters related to the incidence of human diseases, injuries, deformities and defects and the compilation and use of health and vital statistics. Some of the Board's work is carried out in association with international organisations, particularly the World Health Organisation and the EEC.

The Irish Heart Foundation is currently conducting a major research programme, termed 'Mediscan', which aims at preventing coronary heart disease. The Irish Cancer Society, a voluntary body, is devoted to cancer research.

211. The Royal College of Surgeons in Ireland, St Stephen's Green, Dublin.

212. The Central Remedial Clinic, a comprehensive non-residential medical rehabilitation centre whose services are available to persons suffering from any severe physical handicap.

Social Services

With very few exceptions, all employees aged 16 years and over must be covered by social insurance, regardless of the level of their earnings. The cost of insurance is shared by the employer, the employee and the State. The scheme provides for widows', old age, retirement and invalid pensions, unemployment and disability benefits, maternity benefit, death grant and occupational injuries benefit. Benefits are generally flat-rate and comprise a personal allowance and allowances for adult and child dependants. In the case of disability (sickness), unemployment and maternity cash benefits, however, a supplement related to previous earnings is payable in addition to the relevant flat-rate benefit.

Employees who cease to be compulsorily insured may continue to pay voluntary social insurance and receive certain benefits. Contributions paid under Irish social security legislation may be counted, in certain circumstances, to give title to social security benefits in other EEC countries.

People whose means are inadequate and who are not entitled to benefit under the contributory schemes may receive pensions and other benefits from State or other public funds, subject to a means test in some cases. Benefits paid in this way include widows' pensions, unmarried mothers' allowance, deserted wives' allowance, old age pensions, prisoners' wives' allowance, unemployment assistance, blind pensions and allowances for single women aged between 58 and 66.

A means test is not applied in the case of non-contributory children's allowances which are paid to all households in the State in respect of each child, or for the schemes which provide free travel, electricity, fuel, telephone rental and television licences for persons over the age of 66. A country-wide scheme of supplementary welfare allowances and institutional care is provided by local authorities.

Over 100 grant-aided voluntary social service

councils operate throughout the country to co-ordinate the social work of the voluntary organisations in their area. These councils, many of which employ full-time staff, are in turn advised and assisted by a State-sponsored National Social Service Council. This Council is engaged in developing a network of Community Information Centres aimed at informing citizens of health, social welfare and local services available to them.

Communications

Road and Rail Transport

The public road and rail transport system is operated by a State company, CIE (*Córas Iompair Éireann* — the Irish Transport System). The principal cities and towns are linked by rail. Mainline services have been modernised and improved and operate on diesel traction on all lines. Rail freight services have been equipped with the latest technical facilities for the handling and movement of unit-load traffic. CIE also provides special wagons from its own engineering works at Inchicore, Dublin to carry mineral ores and other industrial materials. The total mileage of the rail system at present is approximately 1,250.

CIE also operates a network of bus services including a nation-wide network of fast express routes, the Expressway system, linking major commercial and holiday centres. It provides local commuter services in the cities and large towns as well as long-distance stage carriage bus services, which extend to the more remote areas of the countryside. Road freight transport services, are operated by a number of licensed hauliers located throughout the State. The roads in Ireland are good and relatively uncrowded.

Air Traffic and Airports

Aer Lingus, a State company, which began service in 1936 and is a founder member of the International Air Transport Association (IATA), operates a wide network of air services linking 30 cities in 11 countries. It has a modern jet fleet of Boeing and BAC aircraft. On the transatlantic routes, it operates regular services from Dublin and Shannon to New York, Boston and Chicago. European countries to which *Aer Lingus* flies are Belgium, Denmark, France, Germany, Italy, the Netherlands, Spain, Switzerland and the United Kingdom. In 1978-79, it carried approximately 2,200,000 passengers and 58,000 tons of freight.

Aer Árann Teo., a domestic airline, operates scheduled flights from Galway to the Aran Islands and Dublin. A number of aviation companies

Communications

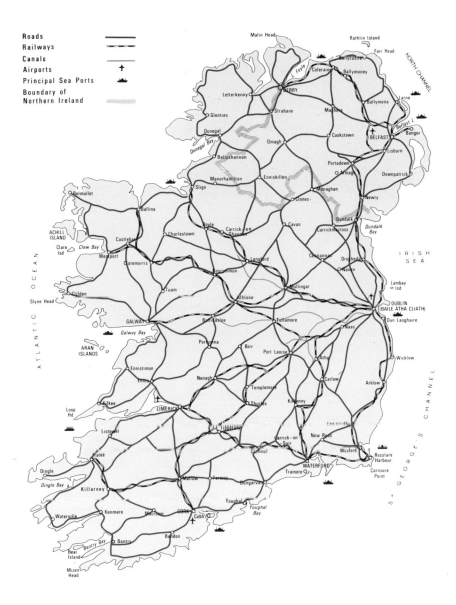

Roads
Railways
Canals
Airports   ✈
Principal Sea Ports   ⛴
Boundary of
Northern Ireland

Malin Head
Rathlin Island
Fair Head
Ballycastle
L. Foyle
Coleraine
Ballymoney
NORTH CHANNEL
Letterkenny
DERRY
Maghera
Ballymena
Larne
Strabane
Belfast L.
Glenties
Cookstown
BELFAST
Bangor
Donegal
Omagh
Lisburn
Donegal Bay
Ballyshannon
Portadown
Downpatrick
Manorhamilton
Enniskillen
Armagh
Belmullet
Clones
Newry
Sligo
Monaghan
Ballina
Dundalk
Boyle
Cavan
Dundalk Bay
Carrick-on-Shannon
Carrickmacross
ACHILL ISLAND
Charlestown
Clare Isd
Clew Bay
Castlebar
Ceannanus
Drogheda
IRISH SEA
Westport
Roscommon
Longford
Navan
Claremorris
Lambay Isd
Clifden
Tuam
Mullingar
Slyne Head
Athlone
DUBLIN (BAILE ATHA CLIATH)
GALWAY
Ballinasloe
Tullamore
Dun Laoghaire
Galway Bay
Naas
ARAN ISLANDS
Portumna
Birr
Wicklow
Ennistimon
Port Laoise
Ennis
Athy
Nenagh
Carlow
Arklow
Loop Hd
Templemore
Kilkenny
Kilkee
Thurles
LIMERICK
Listowel
Enniscorthy
TIPPERARY
Carrick-on-Suir
New Ross
Tralee
Clonmel
Wexford
Rosslare Harbour
Dingle
WATERFORD
Carnsore Point
Mallow
Fermoy
Tramore
Dingle Bay
Dungarvan
Killarney
Youghal
Waterville
Kenmare
Macroom
CORK
Youghal Bay
Cobh
Bantry Bay
Bandon
Bear Island
Bantry
Mizen Head

ATLANTIC OCEAN

ST. GEORGE'S CHANNEL

Scale 1:3,000,000

30 20 10 0   30   60 Km
30   20   10   0   30 Miles

Prepared at the Ordnance Survey Dublin
© Government of Ireland 1978

217

Communications

operates nonscheduled passenger, freight and
helicopter services.

The international airports at Cork, Dublin and
Shannon are managed by *Aer Rianta* on behalf of
the Minister for Transport. Combined passenger
traffic at the three airports is over 4,000,000 a
year. Shannon, the country's transatlantic airport, is
used by major world airlines. The establishment of
Shannon as a customs-free airport in 1947 has
resulted in the development of a thriving industrial
estate in the area.

In addition to the State airports, there are at present
18 private airports which are licensed for
commercial use. The main private airports are those
at Castlebar (Co. Mayo), Oranmore and the Aran
Islands (Co. Galway) and Farranfore (Co. Kerry).
Further private licensed airports are planned.

Shipping
The main ports in Ireland are Arklow, Cork,
Drogheda, Dublin, Dún Laoghaire, Foynes, Galway,
Limerick, New Ross, Rosslare and Waterford. Dublin
and Cork account for over two-thirds of all port
traffic in the country. Slightly less than one-sixth of
tonnage moved is due to coastal trade, about one-
third due to traffic with Britain and the balance
represents trade with other areas.

There are two State-sponsored shipping companies,
Irish Shipping Ltd and the British and Irish Steam
Packet Co. Ltd (B + I Line). The former has a dry
cargo fleet of 159,500 tons deadweight and is
almost exclusively engaged in the deep sea tramping
and chartering trades. A subsidiary of the company,
Irish Continental Lines Ltd, operates a car-ferry
service to France. The B + I line operates passenger
and freight services, including a 'Jet-foil' service, to
Great Britain and freight services to Europe.

Smaller Irish companies are also engaged in the
cross-channel and near-Continental trades.

214

215

Communications

Above: the B + I
symbol.

215. The B + I car
ferry, Leinster,
passing Poolbeg
lighthouse at the
mouth of the river
Liffey.

Postal Telecommunications

The Irish postal and telecommunications services are
at present part of the civil service administered by
the Department of Posts and Telegraphs. The
Government has, however, decided to establish two
separate State-sponsored bodies for the postal and
telecommunications services. As a first step towards
implementing this decision, the Minister for Posts
and Telegraphs has established two interim boards
on a non-statutory basis, one for the postal service
(An Bord Post) and one for the telecommunications
service *(Bord Telecom Éireann)*. Pending enactment
of the necessary legislation for, and the setting up of
permanent bodies to run the two services, which
may take a few years, statutory responsibility for the
postal and telecommunications services remains with
the Minister for Posts and Telegraphs.

When the State-sponsored bodies have been set up,
the residual Ministry will retain responsibility for
general policy matters such as broadcasting, radio,
wireless telegraphy, public policy in relation to posts
and telecommunications, legislation, capital budgets,
etc.

About 90% of all letters mailed reach their
destination within the State on the day following
posting, provided they are mailed by the latest
posting deadline. Mail is delivered once each working
day in country areas and twice in cities and large
towns.

There are about 436,000 telephone exchange lines
and close to 585,000 telephones in Ireland.
Approximately 90% of all subscribers are linked to
the automatic telephone network.

Subscribers in the greater Dublin, Cork, Drogheda,
Dundalk, Galway, Limerick, Shannon and Waterford
areas have direct dialling access to about 45
countries, including most of western Europe and
North America. In addition the majority of
subscribers on the automatic system have direct

Communications

dialling to major centres in the United Kingdom.

The international telex exchange in Dublin was the
first fully electronic stored programme controlled
telex exchange in Europe. The internal telex service
is completely automatic and Irish telex subscribers
have direct access to nearly all countries with
modern automatic systems.

*Above. Symbol of the
Department of Posts
and Telegraphs.*

The Department also supplies the equipment for
computer data to be transmitted over telephone
lines. Data transmission is a relatively new service by
which information is fed to, or obtained from, distant
computers. Data circuits may be either over the
public telephone network or as privately rented direct
lines to a computer.

217

218

217. A view of the
RTE complex at
Donnybrook, Dublin

The Media

Above: Symbol of
Radio Telefís
Éireann.

218. The writer,
Edna O'Brien (left),
recording for the
programme, My
Own Place.

Newspapers and Periodicals

Since the first Irish news sheet appeared in 1659,
there has been a vigorous free press in Ireland.

There are at present seven daily newspapers — five
in Dublin and two in Cork — of which four are
morning papers. The Irish Independent was founded
in 1905 and, with a circulation of about 190,000,
is the largest daily in the country. Independent
Newspapers Ltd group also comprises the *Sunday
World* which has a circulation of about 343,000,
the *Evening Herald* (121,000) and the *Sunday
Independent* (209,000). The *Irish Press* group
comprising the daily *Irish Press* (102,000) and
Evening Press (170,000) and the *Sunday Press*
(396,000) was founded in 1931. *The Irish Times*,
which dates from 1859, has a circulation of about
80,000. The *Cork Examiner*, which was founded in
1854, is now the oldest of the dailies in the State
and has a circulation of about 70,000 mainly in the
southern parts of the country. The same company
also publishes the *Evening Echo* (43,000). Five
Sunday papers are published, the three previously
mentioned and, since 1980, *The Sunday Journal*
and *The Sunday Tribune*. A total of 44 local
newspapers is published in the larger towns in the
provinces, including the oldest extant newspaper in
the State, the *Limerick Chronicle* founded in 1766.

The circulation of the provincial bi-weekly and
weekly newspapers ranges from 7,000 to
44,000, although most of these newspapers have
circulations of 21,000 — 25,000.

In addition there are many periodicals and
magazines, covering a wide range, including
literary, sporting, business, farming and trade
interests.

Radio and Television

The national sound and television broadcasting
service is operated by *Radio Telefís Éireann* (RTE)
an autonomous public corporation, with revenue

derived from licence fees and advertisements. RTE is an active member of the European Broadcasting Union.

There are two colour television channels, the first of which commenced transmission in 1961, and a second which came into operation in 1978. About half of televised material is produced in the RTE studios in Dublin.

Radio broadcasting commenced in 1926 and a second radio channel commenced in 1979. A separate sound service, *Raidio na Gaeltachta*, was established in 1972 to provide a service for the Irish-speaking communities along the west coast and elsewhere in Ireland. In recent years, there has been a considerable development of community broadcasting. The transmitter at Cork provides special programmes for that area. A mobile studio is used to enable people in various parts of the country to make and present their own programmes for broadcast locally on a low-power transmitter.

The broadcasting service maintains a symphony orchestra, a light orchestra and a company of professional actors.

Ireland and the World

International Relations

Ireland in its Constitution affirms its devotion to the ideal of peace and friendly co-operation among nations founded on international justice and morality. Successive Irish Governments have striven to uphold these principles both in their activities in international fora and in their bilateral relations with other countries.

In the United Nations, to which Ireland was admitted in 1955, the Irish delegation has been active in efforts to reduce international tensions and to promote the limitation of arms, particularly nuclear arms. At the same time, the delegation has worked to improve the United Nations peace-keeping rôle and Irish troops have served with distinction in most United Nations peace-keeping missions.

In addition to the United Nations, the following are some of the more important international organisations of which Ireland is a member: Bank for International Settlements, Council of Europe, Food and Agricultural Organisation of the United Nations (FAO), General Agreement on Tariffs and Trade (GATT), International Atomic Energy Agency (IAEA), International Bank for Reconstruction and Development (IBRD, also known as the World Bank), International Civil Aviation Organisation (ICAO), International Development Association (IDA), International Finance Corporation (IFC), International Telecommunications Union (ITU), Organisation for Economic Co-operation and Development (OECD), United Nations Conference on Trade and Development (UNCTAD), United Nations Educational, Scientific and Cultural Organisation (UNESCO), United Nations Universal Postal Union (UPU), World Health Organisation (WHO), World Meteorological Organisation (WMO).

Ireland maintains diplomatic relations with over forty countries. It has close economic and cultural ties with those countries where a significant proportion of the population is of Irish descent such as Australia, Britain, Canada and the United States. It is, however,

International Relations

219. St Patrick's
Hall, Dublin Castle,
prepared for a
meeting during
Ireland's Presidency
of the EEC Council
of Ministers in the
second half of
1979.

natural also that its relations should be particularly close with its European neighbours. Ireland was a founder member of the Council of Europe and has played a prominent part in all its activities.

220. Heads of
Government and
Foreign Ministers of
the Member States
of the EEC in Dublin
in April 1975 during
Ireland's first
Presidency of the
Council of Ministers.

Because of their geographic position, Ireland and Britain have been in close and continuous contact since earliest times. The relationship with Britain since independence has evolved considerably. The participation of both countries in the European Communities has led to increased co-operation in international affairs and, at the same time, the diversification of trade which membership has facilitated has lessened Ireland's traditional economic dependence on Britain.

Together with Britain and Denmark, Ireland became a member of the European Communities on 1 January 1973, after a referendum in which 83% of those who voted had approved the amendment to the Constitution necessary to assume the obligations of membership. Membership of the Community is one of the corner-stones of Irish foreign policy. Ireland has significantly benefited from such Community programmes as the Common Agricultural Policy and the Regional and Social Funds. Within the organs of the Community, Ireland works for the achievement of even closer European integration. Ireland favours the development of the Community institutions and, in particular, the improvement of their decision-making capacity, a representative and effective European Parliament (to which Ireland elects 15 members) and a strong Commission. Ireland also participates in the process of political co-operation among the member-States of the Community which endeavours to formulate common positions on issues of foreign policy facing members.

221

Above: Symbol of the United Nations.

221. Irish UNIFIL soldiers on patrol in Southern Lebanon.

222. Ireland's Permanent Representative to the United Nations, Mr Noel Dorr, chairing a debate in the UN Security Council in April 1981.

222

PRESIDENT   IRELA

Development Co-operation

In recent years, the Irish Government has adopted a planned programme to increase the level of its development aid over a number of years. From IR£800,000 (0.036% of GNP) in 1973, development aid increased to IR£16.226 million (an estimated 0.19% of GNP) in 1980.

In 1980, over 70% of total expenditure on aid to developing countries was channelled through international organisations such as UN agencies (e.g. UNDP and UNICEF), the World Bank, International Development Association, European Communities and the Food Aid Convention, the World Food programme and the International Fertiliser Supply Scheme.

The growth in bilateral aid has been particularly marked, especially in areas such as disaster relief, personal service and project aids in fields where Ireland has a special interest or competence. To ensure that Irish bilateral aid achieves maximum effect, it is mainly concentrated on a limited number of countries. The Agency for Personal Service Overseas (APSO) currently supports over 100 experts and volunteers working in 34 developing countries. Project aid is designed to make available to developing countries the expertise which has been gained by organisations in developing Ireland's own economy. Over thirty State sponsored bodies have combined to form the State Agencies Development Co-operation Organisation (DEVCO) to co-ordinate the development aid activities of its member organisations and to arrange joint projects between them.

As a member of the European Communities, Ireland participates in EEC development co-operation policies. One of the most noteworthy of the EEC's achievements in development co-operation has been the first and second Lomé Conventions, both signed respectively during Ireland's Presidency of the Communities in 1975 and 1979. The Convention extends trade concessions and aid to 59 developing

Development Co-operation

countries in Africa, the Caribbean and the Pacific.

In addition to the official development assistance from Government and State agency funds, money is raised annually by Irish voluntary organisations for development aid projects. In 1980, approximately IR£6 million was raised. This effort is further augmented by the large contribution made to developing countries by an estimated 6,000 Irish lay and religious personnel working in over 60 developing countries.

223. Zebu type cattle in the Sudan. The Agricultural Institute of Ireland is involved in a cross-breeding programme aimed at producing an animal which would yield more milk and mature more rapidly than the local breed. An expansion of this programme is envisaged under the Irish Bilateral Aid Programme as part of a project to establish a dairying co-operative in the Gezira area of the Sudan.

224. In Lesotho a high proportion of scarce land resources has been destroyed by gulley and sheet erosion. The Irish Bilateral Aid Programme is financing an integrated rural development project in Lesotho's Hololo Valley to help solve the problem.

The Irish Abroad

225. The Irish College in Paris, founded in 1578 and the first of a network of some 30 Irish Colleges on the European Continent which extended from Lisbon to Prague. Since the end of the Second World War, it has been leased by the Irish Roman Catholic Bishops to Polish clergy.

226. St Isidore's in Rome, another of the Irish Colleges. It was founded by Luke Wadding OFM (1599-1657).

From the earliest recorded times, the Irish have gone abroad as soldiers, missionaries, traders and emigrants. There were Irish colonies in Wales in the closing years of Roman rule while, from the sixth century, large numbers of Irish settlers gave a Gaelic character to much of Scotland. During the Dark Ages, Ireland remained an isolated centre of Christian culture and Irish monks travelled and settled all over Europe. They founded centres of learning throughout the Continent, many of which flourished for centuries after their foundation.

This first great outward impetus was halted by the internal upheavals caused by the Viking and Norman settlements in Ireland itself. When, in the 17th century, the native polity had been overthrown and religious disabilities introduced, large numbers of Irishman entered the service of most European Continental armies and many rose to the highest ranks. Spain's support for Irish grievances in the 16th century and France's championing of the Stuart cause in the 17th and 18th centuries made these countries, together with Austria, the favoured refuges for Irishmen.

People from many walks of life were active in Europe at this time. Irish merchants settled in Continental ports, Irish doctors and lawyers practised in France, Austria and Spain, while there were Irish protagonists on either side of the major intellectual debates of the 17th century, especially Jansenism. Irish colleges at university centres such as Louvain, Paris, Rome, Lisbon, Salamanca and Alcalá, continued the tradition of Irish scholarship abroad and provided an education for Catholics which was not available at home.

The European period of Irish emigration reached its height in the 18th century, but the French Revolutionary and Napoleonic wars broke many of the Irish links with the Continent, and the granting of Catholic Emancipation lessened the impetus to settle in Europe. Today, however, many Continental

The Irish Abroad

families of Irish origin retain active links with their country of origin.

The movement of Irishmen beyond Europe in appreciable numbers began in the early 18th century. Greater toleration and economic opportunities in the New World attracted many Irishmen, especially Dissenters from Ulster. At first, Pennsylvania was the favoured area for Irish emigrants, but as the century progressed, most east coast cities had large Irish populations. There were large Irish elements in the Revolutionary armies. Four signatories of the American Declaration of Independence were of Irish birth, while another nine were of Irish ancestry.

In the early 19th century, increasing numbers went both to the United States and Canada, but the Great Famine hugely accelerated this emigration. As much as 1% of the population left Ireland for the United States each year between 1840 and 1880. Today, Americans of Irish descent number four times the population of Ireland itself. Irish-Americans are found in all areas of economic, political, public, professional and economic life. Complete integration in American society has not, however, lost these descendants of Irishmen to the culture and aspirations of Ireland and the maintenance of personal and family links is a continuing aspect of the relationship between the two communities.

The European settlement of Australia and New Zealand, begun on a large scale in the 18th and 19th centuries, included many Irishmen who made a considerable impact on the formation and development of these countries.

Numbers of Irishmen settled in rural areas of Argentina in the late 18th and early 19th centuries.

Given the proximity of Ireland to Britain, it is natural that Irishmen at all periods of history made their way to Britain. Emigration there began on a significant

227. Washington's Irish, *a group portrait by Lawrence O'Toole, shows Washington surrounded by 13 men of Irish birth or descent who distinguished themselves in the establishment of the USA. They include four signatories of the Declaration of Independence, the founder of the American Navy and the Secretary of the Continental Congress. The key (above) letters those in the portrait:*

A: *George Washington*
B: *William Irvine*
C: *Richard Montgomery*
D: *Charles Carroll*
E: *John Sullivan*
F: *Thomas Lynch*
G: *James McHenry*
H: *Stephen Moylan*
I: *John Shee*
J: *John Barry*
K: *Edward Hand*
L: *Matthew Thornton*
M: *Richard Butler*
N: *Charles Thomson*

228. Bernardo O'Higgins (1778-1842), son of an Irishman, one of the leading figures in the achievement of the independence of Chile. He was the first head of government there from 1818 to 1823.

229. Charles Gavan Duffy, one of the founders of the Young Ireland Movement, emigrated to Australia in 1855 and later became Prime Minister of Victoria.

230. Thomas D'Arcy McGee, another of the Young Ireland leaders, fled to the United States in 1848 and subsequently became a major figure in Canadian politics.

231. F Scott Fitzgerald, the Irish-American novelist.

232. John F Fitzgerald, the Irish-American Mayor of Boston, in 1910 with his daughter, Rose, mother of President John F Kennedy.

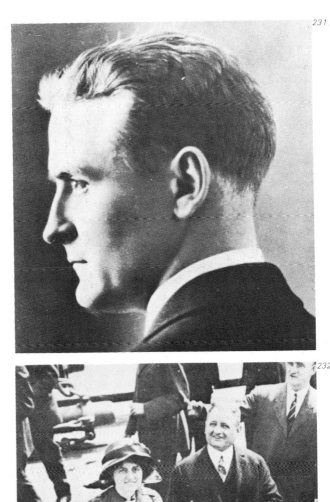

scale in the 18th century when military service and the opportunities opened up by the industrial revolution attracted large numbers. Seasonal migration, especially in the agriculture sector, has also been a feature of the Irish presence in Britain. There are about a million Irish-born people in all walks of life domiciled in Britain to-day, most of whom emigrated in the early postwar years. Persons of Irish birth or descent form a large proportion of the population in Liverpool, Manchester, Glasgow, Birmingham and London.

Irish emigration since the Great Famine took place on a scale so massive as to be unique among modern nations. The reasons for the continuation of emigration are complex but basically they related to the lack of opportunity at home at a time when attractive alternatives were available abroad. While the Irish today take justifiable pride in the contributions which their kinsmen of this and earlier generations have made to so many countries beyond the seas, it was nevertheless keenly felt at home that these contributions were made at Ireland's own expense since all too often it was the young, the able-bodied and the adventurous who left. Since the achievement of independence, successive Governments have worked to create conditions within Ireland which would remove the necessity for emigration. By the mid-sixties the trend had finally been reversed and emigration is no longer considered to be a problem.

The motives for emigration or service abroad have changed also: the broadening of horizons, the search for specialist experience or the voluntary missionary or other humane service to the underdeveloped world. Membership of the EEC has resulted in a renewal of the traditional interchange between Europeans and Irishmen.

Bibliography

Bibliography

This bibliography is intended to provide an introduction to the topics covered. Many of the books listed themselves contain extensive bibliographies. *A Guide to Irish Bibliographical Material* by A Eager (London, Library Association, 1964) can also be used for earlier material.

Books Ireland, a monthly publication available from Goslingstown House, Kilkenny, contains notices of new books and books in print of Irish interest.

Land and People

The Irish Landscape
by GF Mitchell
London, Collins, 1976.

Geology and Scenery in Ireland
by JB Whitlow
London, Penguin, 1975.

The Climate of Ireland
by PK Rohan
Dublin, Stationery Office, 1975.

Ireland
by T Sheehy
Gill and Macmillan, 1979.

The Geography of Ireland
by JP Haughton and DA Gillmor
Dublin, Department of Foreign Affairs, 1979.

A Natural History of Ireland
by C Moriarty
Cork, Mercier Press, 1972.

Census Catalogue of the Flora of Ireland
by MJO Scannell and DM Synnott
Dublin, Stationery Office, 1972.

The Fauna of Ireland
by F O'Rourke
Cork, Mercier Press, 1970.

An Irish Beast Book
by JS Fairley
Belfast, Blackstaff press, 1974.

A List of the Birds of Ireland
by RF Ruttledge
Dublin, Stationery Office, 1976.

Bibliography

Freshwater Life in Ireland
by CS Woods
Shannon, Irish University Press, 1974.

Census of Population of Ireland 1971
Dublin, Stationery Office, 1971 sqq. 8 vols.

Social Statistics in Ireland, a guide to their sources and uses
by J McGilvray
Dublin, Institute of Public Administration, 1977.

Bibliography of Irish Family History and Genealogy
by B De Breffny
Cork, Mercier Press, 1974.

Irish Historiography 1934-1968
edited by TW Moody
Dublin, Royal Irish Academy, 1972.

The Irish World
edited by B de Breffny
London, Thames and Hudson, 1977.

The Course of Irish History
edited by FX Martin and TW Moody
Cork, Mercier Press, 1967.

A Short History of Ireland
by JC Beckett
London, Hutchinson, 1966.

The Celtic Realms
by M Dillon and N Chadwick
London, Weidenfeld and Nicolson, 1967.

Ireland before the Vikings
by G Mac Niocail
Dublin, Gill and Macmillan, 1972.

Ireland before the Normans
by D Ó Corráin
Dublin, Gill and Macmillan, 1972.

Anglo-Norman Ireland
by M Dolley
Dublin, Gill and Macmillan, 1972.

Gaelic and Gaelicised Ireland in the Later Middle Ages
by K Nicholls
Dublin, Gill and Macmillan, 1972.

Bibliography

Early Modern Ireland 1534-1691:
A New History of Ireland, vol III
edited by TW Moody, FX Martin and FJ Byrne
London, Oxford University Press, 1976.

The Making of Modern Ireland 1603-1921
by JC Beckett
London, Faber and Faber, 1966.

Ireland since the Famine
by FSL Lyons
London, Weidenfeld and Nicolson, 1971.

The Green Flag: a history of Irish nationalism
by R Kee
London, Weidenfeld and Nicolson, 1972.

The Irish State

Ireland in the Twentieth Century
by JA Murphy
Dublin, Gill and Macmillan, 1975.

Constitution of Ireland
Dublin, Stationery Office, 1937.

The Government and Politics of Ireland
by B Chubb
London, Oxford University Press, 1974.

The Irish Parliamentary Tradition
by B Farrell
Dublin, Gill and Macmillan, 1973.

The Houses of the Oireachtas
by J McGowan Smyth
Dublin, Institute of Public Adminsitration, 1973.

Guide to the 21st Dáil and Seanad
by Ted Nealon, written in association with Frank Dunlop
Dublin, Platform Press, 1977.

The Administration of Justice in Ireland
by VTH Delaney (edited by C Lysaght)
Dublin, Institute of Public Administration, 1975.

The Irish Civil Service
by S Dooney
Dublin, Institute of Public Administration, 1976.

Bibliography

Guardians of the Peace
by C Brady
Dublin, Gill and Macmillan, 1974.

Northern Ireland

Northern Ireland 1921-1974: a select bibliography
London, Garland Prior, 1976.

The Ulster Question 1603-1973
by TW Moody
Cork, Mercier Press, 1974.

Northern Ireland 1968-1974: a chronology of events
by R Deutsch and V Magowan
Belfast, Blackstaff, 1973-1975, 3 vols.

Governing without Consensus
by R Rose
London, Faber and Faber, 1971.

Conflict in Northern Ireland
by J Darby
Dublin, Gill and Macmillan, 1976.

Northern Ireland: a political directory 1968-1978
by WD Flackes
Dublin, Gill and Macmillan, 1980.

The Ulster Year Book
Belfast, HMSO, 1981.

Northern Ireland— All the places to stay
Northern Ireland Tourist Board, 1981.

Northern Ireland
Northern Ireland Tourist Board, 1981.

Culture

A View of the Irish Language
edited by B Ó Cuiv
Dublin, Stationery Office, 1969.

The Irish Language
by D Greene
Cork, Mercier Press/The Cultural Relations Committee
Ireland, 1966.

Bibliography

English — Irish Dictionary
edited by T de Bhaldraithe
Dublin, Stationery Office, 1959.

Foclóir Gaeilge — Béarla (Irish — English Dictionary)
edited by N Ó Dónaill
Dublin, Stationery Office, 1978.

Irish Folkways
by EE Evans
London, Routledge & Kegan Paul, 1957.

The Folklore of Ireland
by S Ó Súilleabháin
London, Batsford, 1974.

Storytelling in Irish Tradition
by S Ó Súilleabháin
Cork, Mercier Press/The Cultural Relations Committee of
Ireland, 1973.

Dictionary of Irish Writers
compiled by B Cleeve
Cork, Mercier Press, 1967-1971, 3 vols.

A Literary History of Ireland
by D Hyde, a new edition with an introduction by B Ó Cuív
London, Benn, 1967.

Literature in Irish
by P Mac Cana
Dublin, Department of Foreign Affairs, 1980.

Gaelic Literature Surveyed
by A de Blácam
Dublin, Talbot Press, 1972.

Filíocht Ghaeilge na Linne Seo
by Frank O'Brien
Dublin, An Clóchomhar, 1968.

Seven Centuries of Irish Learning 1000-1700
by B Ó Cuív
Cork, Mercier Press, 1971.

Writing in Irish Today
by D Greene
Cork, Mercier Press/The Cultural Relations Committee of
Ireland, 1972.

Anglo-Irish Literature
by Augustine Martin
Dublin, Department of Foreign Affairs, 1980.

Bibliography

Select Bibliography for the Study of Anglo-Irish Literature and
its Background, Irish Studies Handbook
by M Harmon
Dublin, Wolfhound, 1977.

Irish Poets in English
edited by S Lucy
Cork, Mercier Press, 1972.

Swift, The Man, His Works and the Age
by I Ehrenpreis
London, Methuen, 1962-1967, 3 vols.

Oliver Goldsmith, His Life and Works
by A Lython Sells
London, George Allen & Unwin, 1974.

Oscar Wilde
by H Montgomery Hyde
London, Eyre Methuen, 1976.

Ireland's Literary Renaissance
by EA Boyd
New York, Barnes and Noble, 1967.

Theatre in Ireland
by M Ó hAodha
Oxford, Blackwell, 1974.

Yeats: The Man and the Masks
by R Ellmann
London, Faber and Faber, 1973.

WB Yeats: The Critical Heritage
edited by AN Jeffares
London, Routledge & Kegan Paul, 1976.

Shaw: The Critical Heritage
by TF Evans
London, Routledge & Kegan Paul, 1975.

Synge, a critical study of the plays
by N Greene
London, Macmillan, 1976.

James Joyce
by R Ellmann
New York, Oxford University Press, 1965.

Seán O'Casey and his World
by D Krause
London, Thames and Hudson, 1976.

Flann O'Brien, a critical introduction
by A Clissman
Dublin, Gill and Macmillan, 1975.

Bibliography

The Irish Novel in Our Time
by P Rafroidi and M Harmon
Lille, L'université de Lille, 1976.

Samuel Beckett
by J Pilling
London, Routledge & Kegan Paul, 1976.

Two Decades of Irish Writing. A Critical Anthology
edited by D Dunn
Cheshire, Carcanet Press, 1975.

Northern Voices
by T Brown
Dublin, Gill and Macmillan, 1976.

The National Gallery of Ireland
by J White
London, Thames and Hudson, 1968.

A Dictionary of Irish Artists
by W Strickland
Dublin, 1913; reprinted Wakekeld, EP Publishing, 1976, 2 vols.

A Concise History of Irish Art
by B Arnold
London, Thames and Hudson, 1976.

Early Irish Art
by Máire de Paor
Dublin, Department of Foreign Affairs, 1979.

Early Christian Irish Art
by F Henry
Cork, Mercier Press/The Cultural Relations Committee of Ireland, 1980.

Treasures of Ireland, Irish pagan and early christian art
by F Henry
London, Thames and Hudson, 1965-1970, 3 vols.

Irish Art from 1000
by A O Crookshank
Dublin, Department of Foreign Affairs, 1979.

Painters of Ireland 1660-1860
by A Crookshank and the Knight of Glin
London, Barrie and Jenkins, 1978.

Irish Portraits 1660-1860
by A Crookshank and the Knight of Glin
Dublin, National Gallery, 1969.

Bibliography

Irish Art in the Nineteenth Century
Dublin, National Gallery, 1971.

Jack B Yeats
by H Pyle
London, RHK, 1970.

Irish Art 1900-1950
Cork, Municipal Gallery, 1975.

Art in Ulster: 1
by J Hewitt
Belfast, Blackstaff Press, 1977.

Art in Ulster: 2
by M Catto
Belfast, Blackstaff Press, 1977.

Irish Glass, the age of exuberance
by P Warren
London, Faber and Faber, 1970.

Irish Stained Glass
by J White and M Wynne
Dublin, Gill, 1963.

Irish Silver
by R Wyse-Jackson
Cork, Mercier Press, 1972.

Guide to the National Monuments in the Republic of Ireland
by P Harbison
Dublin, Gill and Macmillan, 1975.

Architecture in Ireland
by M Craig
Dublin, Department of Foreign Affairs, 1979.

The Churches and Abbeys of Ireland
by B de Breffny and G Mott
London, Thames and Hudson, 1976.

Architecture and Sculpture in Ireland 1150-1350
by RA Stalley
Dublin, Gill and Macmillan, 1971.

Irish Houses and Castles
by D Guinness and W Ryan
London, Thames and Hudson, 1971.

Irish Classic Houses of the Middle Size
by M Craig
London, Architectural Press, 1976.

Bibliography

An Introduction to Ulster Architecture
by H Dixon
Belfast, Ulster Architectural Society, 1976.

Ireland's Vernacular Architecture
by K Danaher
Cork, Mercier Press/The Cultural Relations Committee of Ireland, 1975.

A Catalogue of Contemporary Irish Composers
Cork, Mercier Press, 1976.

Anglo-Irish Music 1780-1830
by M Hogan
Cork University Press, 1966.

Carolan, the life and times of an Irish harper
by D O'Sullivan
London, Routledge & Kegan Paul, 1958, 2 vols.

The Life and Music of John Field
by P Pigott
London, Faber and Faber, 1973.

The Irish Song Tradition
by S O'Boyle
Dublin, O'Brien Press, 1976.

Folk Music and Dances of Ireland
by B Breathnach
Cork, Mercier Press, 1978.

Irish Folk Music, Song and Dance
by D O'Sullivan
Cork, Mercier Press/The Cultural Relations Committee of Ireland, 1977.

The Irish Harp
by J Rimmer
Cork, Mercier Press/The Cultural Relations Committee of Ireland, 1977.

Sport in Ireland
by N Carroll
Dublin, Department of Foreign Affairs, 1979.

Camán: 2,000 years of hurling in Ireland
by A Ó Maolfabhaill
Dundalk, Dundalgan Press, 1973.

The Bass Book of Irish Soccer
by S Ryan and N Dunne
Cork, Mercier Press, 1975.

Bibliography

One Hundred Years of Irish Rugby
by E Van Esbeck
Dublin, Gill and Macmillan, 1974.

Sailing Around Ireland
by W Clarke
London, Batsford, 1976.

Hunting in Ireland
by CA Lewis
London, Allen, 1975.

Economy

An Economic History of Ireland since 1600
by LM Cullen
London, Batsford, 1972.

The Irish Economy since 1922
by J Meenan
Liverpool, University Press, 1970.

Economic Growth in Ireland: the experience since 1947
by KA Kennedy and B Dowling
Dublin, Gill and Macmillan, 1975.

The Economy of Ireland
edited by J O'Hagan
Dublin, Irish Management Institute, 1976.

Irish Industry: Structure and Performance
by P O O'Malley
Dublin, Gill and Macmillan, 1971.

Regional and Industrial Development Trends in Ireland
by PN O'Farrell
Dublin, Institute of Public Administration, 1975.

The Rise of Irish Trade Unionism
by A Boyd
Tralee, Anvil, 1972.

The Decade of Upheaval: Irish Trade Unions in the
Nineteen Sixties
by C McCarthy
Dublin, Institute of Public Administration, 1973.

Currency and Central Banking in Ireland
by M Moynihan
Dublin, Gill and Macmillan, 1975.

Bibliography

Ireland Guide
Dublin, Bord Fáilte Éireann, 1981.

Services

A Law for the Poor: a study of home assistance in Ireland
by S Ó Cinnéide
Dublin, Institute of Public Administration, 1970.

The Health Services of Ireland
by B Hensey
Dublin, Institute of Public Administration, 1979.

The Irish Education and Training Directory
by N Casey and N Murray
Claremorris, Careers and Education Publications, 1976.

A Mirror to Kathleen's Face: education in independent Ireland
1922-1960
by DH Akenson
Dublin, O'Brien Press, 1976.

Post-Primary Education in Ireland 1957-1970
by E Randles
Dublin, Veritas, 1976.

Communication Policies in Ireland
by J Stapleton
Paris, UNESCO, 1974.

Travel and Transport in Ireland
by KB Nowlan
Dublin, Gill and Macmillan, 1973.

Written on the Wind: personal memories of Irish radio,
1926-1976
edited by L McRedmond
Dublin, Gill and Macmillan, 1976.

Ireland and the World

The Formulation of Irish Foreign Policy
by P Keatinge
Dublin, Institute of Public Administration, 1973.

A Place Among the Nations: Issues in Irish Foreign Policy
by P Keatinge
Dublin, Institute of Public Administration, 1978.

255

Bibliography

Spanish Knights of Irish Origin
edited by M Walsh
Dublin, Stationery Office, 1961-64, 3 vols.

Biographical Dictionary of Irishmen in France
by P Hayes
Dublin, Gill, 1949.

Ulster Emigration to Colonial America
by RJ Dickson
London, Rutledge & Kegan Paul, 1966.

The American Irish
by WV Shannon
New York, Macmillan, 1963.

The Irish Exiles in Australia
by TJ Kiernan
Dublin, Clonmore and Reynolds, 1954.

The Irish in Britain
by K O'Connor
Dublin, Gill and Macmillan, 1972.

Credits

The Department of Foreign Affairs wishes to express its appreciation to the following for photographs used in this Book:

Photograph number	Source
2, 3, 4, 5, 7, 8, 9, 12, 27, 32, 46, 73, 86, 113, 115, 132, 133, 137, 138, 139, 140, 141, 144, 157, 167, 168, 170, 171, 172, 176, 191, 200, 201, 202, 204, 211	Bord Fáilte Éireann
37, 38, 39, 40, 44, 47, 48, 93, 94, 95, 96, 100, 119, 120, 121, 122, 123, 124, 147, 149	National Gallery of Ireland
1, 10, 11, 13, 66, 67, 68, 69, 112, 114, 116, 130, 131, 135, 219	Office of Public Works
14, 15, 16, 17, 25, 29, 30, 33, 35, 72, 81, 173, 174, 179, 214	Photocraft AV
41, 43, 45, 51, 57, 148, 228, 229, 230	National Library of Ireland
108, 109, 110, 111, 118, 143	National Museum of Ireland
49, 50, 65, 78, 90, 99, 102, 104	The Irish Times
145, 177, 181, 182, 183, 184, 186, 188, 189, 198	Industrial Development Authority
158, 159, 160, 161, 162	Institute of Industrial Research and Standards
77, 125, 126, 127, 128	Bank of Ireland (photos by John Donat and James G. Maguire)
18, 19, 20, 21, 22, 23, 24, 26	Éamon de Buitléar
53, 193, 194, 195, 197	Electricity Supply Board
37, 154, 156, 217, 218	Radio Telefis Éireann
53, 59, 91, 221	Irish Press
31, 165, 166, 169	Ruth Rogers
54, 220	Cliché Photothèque CEE, DG de l'Information
39, 150, 151	Claddagh Records Ltd.
206, 207, 208	Green Studio
223, 224	An Foras Talúntais
203, 209	A + D Wejehert
63, 164	Jim Connolly

Credits

Credits